Catho...
Jewish Relations

Documents from the Holy See

INTRODUCTION BY DR. EUGENE J. FISHER

All CTS booklets
are published thanks to the
generous support of its Members

CATHOLIC TRUTH SOCIETY
PUBLISHERS TO THE HOLY SEE

CONTENTS

© 1999 The Incorporated Catholic Truth Society
40-46 Harleyford Road
London SE11 5AY

Tel: (0171) 640 0042 Fax: (0171) 640 0046

ISBN 1 86082 062 X

Cover: *Chief Rabbi of Rome and Pope John Paul II, April 1996.*
Courtesy of the Study Centre for Christian-Jewish Relations.

PREFACE

In this our time the catechetical need to offer guidance on Catholic-Jewish relations is as pressing and necessary as ever. The gathering of the documents of the Holy See into one booklet, together with the studied comments of Dr Fisher, will prove to be of enormous value for the study of the development of understanding between the Jewish people and Catholics. It should promote a greater awareness of Catholic duty and responsibility, enable us to set in context the historical picture which promotes the change of attitude needed to discover the truth. It will help all of us to recognise the need for genuine repentance which is fitting as we approach the Holy Year of the Great Jubilee.

✚ Charles J. Henderson

Chairman for the Committee for Catholic-Jewish Relations of the Episcopal Conferences of England and Wales.

INTRODUCTION

THE EVOLUTION OF A TRADITION: THE DOCUMENTS OF THE HOLY SEE ON CATHOLIC-JEWISH RELATIONS

by Eugene J. Fisher

The four documents included in this booklet constitute the entire corpus of universal Roman Catholic teaching on Jews and Judaism since the close of the apostolic period.[1] While much was said about these subjects by Popes and councils over the centuries (some of it negative, some, albeit less, positive), those statements were disciplinary in character, not doctrinal. Cardinal Johannes Willebrands, who worked on *Nostra Aetate* with his predecessor Cardinal Bea during the Council, frequently cited the uniqueness of *Nostra Aetate* no. 4 as the only text of the Second Vatican Council devoid of any reference to earlier councils, or to patristic or papal teachings. *Nostra Aetate*, Willebrands asserted, represented the first systematic, doctrinally relevant statement on the Church's relationship with the Jewish people in Catholic history.[2]

It is, sadly, most likely that the reason that neither Popes nor councils in earlier centuries felt called upon to debate and decree officially on the Church's doctrinal position with regard to Judaism was that the negative portrait of Judaism painted by the early Church fathers was so widely presumed by later Christians

1 The Dogmatic Constitutions of the Church, *Lumen Gentium*, no. 16, and *Dei Verbum*, no's. 15-16 also contain relevant statements affirming central aspects of the teaching of the Declaration, *Nostra Aetate* no. 4.

2 Johannes Cardinal Willebrands, *Church and the Jewish People: New Considerations* (New York/Mahwah, 1992) p. 40.

that no one thought to question what in our time has aptly been called "the teaching of contempt."[3] The four statements presented here, then, represent the sum and substance of official Catholic teaching on Jews and Judaism, a definitive utterance of the Magisterium binding on the presentation of the Catholic faith by catechists and homilists alike.

While these statements have no true doctrinal precedent in Catholic Tradition, however, they do have a wider magisterial context today in the statements of the Popes[4] and of local Churches since the Second Vatican Council. These can provide most useful insights for interpreting and applying the Church-wide documents included here.

The title of this introduction is taken from a longer paper[5] that I was invited by the Holy See to give at a meeting of the International Catholic-Jewish Liaison Committee in 1986 analysing the development of the then three official statements of the Commission for Religious Relations with the Jews: the Conciliar text and the Commission's two implementing documents

3 The term, "teaching of contempt," was coined by the great French Jewish historian, Jules Isaac, to describe the overall effect of Patristic polemics against Jews and Judaism. Isaac's 1960 meeting with Pope John XXIII resulted in the Pope mandating that the Council take up the topic. Cf. Jules Isaac, *The Teaching of Contempt* (1964) and *Jesus and Israel* (1971), both translated and introduced by Claire Huchet Bishop for Holt, Rinehart, Winston.

4 The statements of Pope John Paul II have been collected in Spiritual Pilgrimage: *Texts on Jews and Judaism* 1979-1995, edited by Eugene Fisher and Leon Klenicki (New York: Crossroad, 1995).

5 Eugene Fisher, "The Evolution of Tradition from *Nostra Aetate* to the Notes," in International Catholic-Jewish Liaison Committee, *Fifteen years of Catholic-Jewish Dialogue*, 1970-1985 (Libreria editrice Vaticana/Libreria Editrice Lanteranense, 1988) pp. 239-254. An expanded version of the paper is available in E. Fisher and L. Klenicki, *In Our Time*: The *Flowering of Catholic-Jewish Dialogue* (N.Y./Mahwah: Paulist Press, 1990).

5

of 1974 and 1985. The most recent document of the Commission, *We Remember, A Reflection on the Shoah*, like its three predecessors, was greeted with initial scepticism and critiques by Jewish and even Catholic commentators. Great concern was expressed in 1965, for example, that *Nostra Aetate* failed to mention the term, "deicide," and that it "deplored" rather than "condemned" anti-Semitism. The former term, it was feared, might someday creep back into Christian vocabulary, while the sinfulness of anti-Semitism might not be clear in the use of the latter.[6]

Yet over time, these understandable concerns and fears have been allayed as it became apparent that the Church has turned itself irrevocably unto a course of replacing the ancient negative attitude toward Jews and Judaism with a positive, even fraternal one of mutual respect and solidarity with the Jewish people and the even more ancient faith given them by God. In 1974, the Vatican Guidelines summarized the Conciliar text as having 'condemned' anti-Semitism, while in 1986, Pope John Paul II declared anti-Semitism to be 'sinful'.[7] It is an interesting irony that when I started working in this field a quarter of a century ago I could not give a talk to a Catholic group without defining what I meant by the word, Holocaust.

6 Examples of concerns expressed with regard to the 1974 and 1985 texts are given in *Fifteen Years* and *In Our Time*, cf. supra.

7 John Paul II, 26 Nov. 1986, *Spiritual Pilgrimage*, p. 83: "For the Jewish People themselves, Catholics should have not only respect but also great fraternal love for it is the teaching of both the Hebrew Scriptures and Christian Scriptures that the Jews are beloved of God, who has called them with irrevocable calling. No valid theological justification could ever be found for acts of discrimination or persecution against the Jews. In fact, such acts must be held to be sinful." The 1998 Vatican document, *We Remember* similarly places anti-Semitism (and crimes motivated by it) in the category of very serious sins committed over the centuries by members of the Church not individually but institutionally as well.

6

Today, 'Holocaust' is part of the working vocabulary of our culture, and thanks to the most recent Vatican document, *Shoah* will be. But the term, 'deicide', has virtually passed from usage among Catholics, so it, now, is the term I must define.

Such progressive clarifications of the doctrinal and catechetical intent of the Conciliar declaration, *Nostra Aetate* are what I mean by the term 'evolution of a tradition'. The dynamic that drives this process toward an ever more positive appreciation of Judaism and its ongoing role in the mystery of salvation, of course, is dialogue. It is a dialogue that has taken place since the Council not only at the top, between the Holy See's Commission and the International Jewish Committee for Interreligious Relations, but on all levels of the life of the Church and the Jewish People. In the U.S., and increasingly elsewhere as well, there have been national dialogues, diocesan-level dialogues, and congregational level dialogues, nurturing and 'enfleshing' the teaching documents issued by the Holy See and intended for the guidance of the whole Church.

The documents included here, then, reflect not only a dialogue between the Church and the Jewish people, but equally a dialogue within the Church as well, since they draw upon, reflect, and in turn affirm statements made at the level of national episcopal conferences and dioceses throughout the world. One may say without exaggeration that the amazing progress in Catholic-Jewish relations since the Second Vatican Council is a classic example of how the Conciliar vision has been received and implemented over time. Catholics, I believe, owe a tremendous debt of gratitude to those Jews who, despite the deep trauma of the *Shoah* (one out of every three Jews in the world and two out of every three in Europe were systematically

7

murdered, mostly by people who, if they cannot be called Christian, at least were baptized as such), have come forward to participate in these sometimes very painful dialogues with us. Indeed, as Pope John Paul II told the tiny remnant of the once thriving Jewish community of Warsaw in 1987, theirs is a 'saving warning'[8] and 'sacred witness' to the Church and the world alike.

The 1985 Vatican Notes, it should be emphasized, also speak of the ongoing witness of the Jewish people that is theirs alone and not exhausted in Judaism's role of preparing the way for the first coming of Christ: 'The history of Israel did not end in 70 A.D. (Cf.. Guidelines, II). It continued, especially in a numerous Diaspora which allowed Israel to carry to the whole world a witness - often heroic - of its fidelity to the one God and to exalt him in the presence of all the living (Tobit 13:4).' 'Heroic witness' is the precise meaning of the term, 'martyrdom'. Over the centuries, we know, many of the persecutors of Jews who martyred so many of God's people were active Christians.

On the one hand, the Pope and the Holy See's Commission are here inviting all Catholics to contemplate and repent for crimes against Jews as Jews committed by Christians on all levels of the Church. On the other hand, they are making, in direct continuity with the Second Vatican Council[9], a doctrinal assertion the implications of which may take centuries to unfold. The Jewish witness to the world is intrinsic to the ongoing status of the Jewish people as divinely chosen, i.e. as the people of God of the Old Covenant

8 John Paul II, Pastoral Visit to Poland, June 14, 1987. *Spiritual Pilgrimage*, p. 99.

9 Cf. not only *Nostra Aetate* no. 4, but also *Lumem Gentium*, no. 16.

which has never been revoked.[10] This status has endured over the centuries and, according to Catholic teaching, will endure until the end of time.[11] The chosenness and the saving witness of the Jews to the Church and to the world, therefore, was not exhausted in its role of preparing the way for Christ's first coming, but is integral in itself and to be respected by the Church as a proclamation of revealed truth in its own right. This is why the Pope during his 1986 visit to the Great Synagogue of Rome, and the joint documents here speak of the 'joint witness' of the church and the Jewish people to the world based on revelation itself.[12] The 1985 notes, speaking in the context of the eschatological dimension of our shared proclamation, urge us to 'a greater awareness that the people of God of the Old and the New Testament are tending towards a like end in the future, the coming or the return of the Messiah, even if they start from two different points of view... Attentive to the same God who has spoken, hanging on the same word, we have to witness to one same memory and one common hope in Him who is the master of history. We must also accept our responsibility to prepare the world for the coming of the Messiah by working together for social justice, respect for the rights of persons and nations, and for social and international reconciliation. To this we are driven, Jews and Christians, by the command to love our neighbour, by a common hope for the Kingdom of God and by the great heritage of the prophets'.[13]

10 This phrase, first spoken by Pope John Paul II in his allocution to the Jewish community of Mainz on 17 Nov. 1980, was reaffirmed by the 1985 Vatican *Notes* as a "remarkable theological formula" which establishes the "the permanent reality of the Jewish people" as a "living reality closely related to the church."
11 Cf. the 1985 *Notes*, no's. 2. 3, 10, 11, 25.
12 *Spiritual Pilgrimage*, p. 65.
13 1985 *Notes*, no. 11.

Finally, a few words need to be said about the 1998 document, *We Remember: A Reflection on the Shoah*. Like the three which preceded it, *We Remember* was greeted cautiously, and by some in the Jewish community negatively. Again, ambiguities in language were noted, and again it was feared that the worst possible interpretation of anything vague would in the long run prevail. But as with the Council itself and the two previous implementing documents of the Holy See in 1974 and 1985, I would suggest that this document's actual impact on Catholic understanding, will be positive. What will last is not what the document failed to say (which was the focus of much of the Jewish critique) but what it did say, and say very powerfully.[14]

It is also important to note that the document now has received an official interpretation in the light of Jewish concerns by Cardinal Edward I. Cassidy, who signed it as president of the Pontifical Commission which issued it. Cardinal Cassidy's definitive interpretation[15], for example, clarifies both the distinction and the causal relationship between ancient Christian anti-Judaism and modern racial anti-Semitism. The distinction is clear. Christian anti-Judaism was a form of theological triumphalism held in check by its own theoretical foundations as well as the Church's moral restraints (as can be found already in St. Augustine and in the legislation of Pope Gregory the Great which afforded Jews a legal place in Christian society and

14 Cardinal Cassidy in his reflection on the document cites a number of Jewish commentators who have made this and similar positive points. See *Catholics Remember*, pp. 68-69.

15 It has been published in *Origins* and *Catholic International*, as well as in the collection of statements on the *Shoah* of the Bishops' Conferences of Hungary, Germany, Poland, The U.S., Holland, Switzerland, France, Italy and the Holy See. See *Catholics Remember the Holocaust* (Washington, DC: National Conference of Catholic Bishops, 1998) pp. 61-76.

10

Judaism alone the right to exist as a non-Christian religion). Modern anti-Semitism, on the other hand, found its theoretical base in a post-enlightenment, pseudo-scientific racialism set in an ideology (Nazism) that was every bit as opposed in theory to Christianity and the Church as it was to Judaism, though in practice the chilling decision was made, consciously and with infinite malice, to destroy the first witnesses to God's first Covenant, the Jews.

What is admittedly less clear in the document, though clearly implicit in the structure of the relevant sections, is that while Christian anti-Judaism differed profoundly from racial anti-Semitism in theory and in the practices that flowed from those theories.[16] Christian anti-Judaism did pave the way for the successful spread of anti-Semitism through a populace that Christian teaching had for centuries pinpointed as an 'alien other' in Christian society, and one whose moral failings, beginning with falsely alleged collective guilt for Jesus' death, were many and frightening to the people. Thus, by the 20th Century all too many Christians were ripe to fall into the temptation that Nazi anti-Semitism offered to blame all of society's ills on 'the Jews'. The Vatican document thus cites the words of Pope John Paul II: 'In the Christian world... erroneous and unjust interpretations of the New Testament regarding the Jewish People and their alleged culpability have circulated for too long, engendering feelings of hostility toward these people.' These negative feelings fed by Christian anti-Judaism in turn, the Pope stated, 'lulled the consciences' of

16 In almost two millennia Christianity never attempted anything like a systematic destruction of the Jewish people as such. The word "genocide" is a modern coinage developed specifically to describe what happened to the Jews of Europe in the 20th Century, a new word never felt to be necessary before, though used in a wide variety of contexts today.

11

many Christians so that they did not act towards the Jews 'as the world had the right to expect' Christians to act when their time of testing came.[17] Put another way, Christian anti-Judaism was a necessary cause of the Holocaust, but not a sufficient cause. Without it, the Holocaust would most probably never have happened. But a number of other causes, sociological, economic, historical and ideological are necessary even to approach a 'sufficient' explanation for what happened.

Cardinal Cassidy also clarified another vital point in the text. In quoting the Pope in the passage cited above, the Vatican document naturally included a phrase that the Pope had used, 'I do not say the Church as such was guilty.' And in making its statement of the need for universal repentance by the Church, the document used the phrase 'the failures of her (the Church's) sons and daughters in every age.' This lead some commentators to conclude that the document intended to exculpate the institutional Church in the former, and the hierarchy in the latter.

This was not at all the intent of the document, Cardinal Cassidy affirmed. Rather, the use of the phrase was meant to distinguish the Church as a human institution (with its need for repentance without reservation) from the Church as a sacrament, the locus of the encounter between Christ and the communion of the baptized, living and dead, past, present and future. 'For Catholics the Church is not just the members that belong to it. It is looked upon as the bride of Christ, the heavenly Jerusalem, holy and sinless. We do not speak of the Church as sinful but of the members of the Church as sinful.' Likewise, he reminded his audience, 'sons and daughters' excludes

17 John Paul II, Symposium on the Roots of Anti-Judaism, 31 Oct 1997, *L'Osservatore Romano* (1 Nov 1997): 6, no. 1.

no one, but, like the term, members, 'can include according to circumstances Popes, Cardinals, Bishops, priests, and laity.' So one can, according to the Vatican document, indict the Church as a human institution on all levels for its sins of omission and of comission with regard to the Jews over the course of the centuries and during the *Shoah* itself.

Indeed, one must say that such an interpretation is the central point of the entire exercise undertaken in the document, as the document ringingly concludes: 'At the end of the millennium the Catholic Church desires to express her deep sorrow for the failures of her sons and daughters in every age. This is an act of repentance *(teshuvah)*, since as members of the Church we are linked to the sins as well as the merits of all her children... It is not a matter of mere words but of binding commitment... Humanity cannot permit all that *(the Shoah)* to happen again. We pray that our sorrow for the tragedy which the Jewish people has suffered in our century will lead to a new relationship with the Jewish people. We wish to turn awareness of past sins into a firm resolve to build a new future in which there will be no more anti-Judaism among Christians... but rather a shared mutual respect as befits those who adore the one Creator and the Lord and have a common father in faith, Abraham.'

In a statement on the implications of the document issued from Rome by Cardinal William Keeler and myself the day after its promulgation, we drew out two critical mandates for its implementation in local Churches around the world:

First, we must commit our resources, our historians, sociologists, theologians and other scholars, to study together with their Jewish counterparts all the evidence with a view to a healing of memories, a reconciliation of history. Second, we must look at the implications of this document for our educational programs, its opportunities for rethinking old categories as well as probing the most difficult areas of moral thought. To take the Holocaust seriously is to look back at centuries of Christian misunderstandings both of Judaism and of the New Testament itself, as the text emphasizes, and seek to replace them with more accurate appreciations of both. How shall we embody what this statement calls us to do in our classrooms and from our pulpits?[18]

18 See *Catholics Remember*, p. 57

Dr. Eugene J. Fisher

Associate Director, Secretariat for Ecumenical and Interreligious Affairs, National Conference of Catholic Bishops (U.S.A.)

Washington, D.C. Lent, 1999

14

1. DECLARATION ON THE RELATIONSHIPS OF THE CHURCH TO NON-CHRISTIAN RELIGIONS

(NOSTRA AETATE (NO. 4) (OCTOBER 28, 1965)

ECUMENICAL COUNCIL VATICAN II

Paul, Bishop
Servant of the Servants of God
Together with the Fathers of the Sacred Council
For everlasting memory

Declaration on the relation of the Church to non-Christian Religions.

1. Preamble

In our time, when day by day mankind is being drawn closer together, and the ties between different peoples are becoming stronger, the Church examines more closely her relationship to non-Christian religions. In her task of promoting unity and love among men, indeed among nations, she considers above all in this declaration what men have in common and what draws them to fellowship.

One is the community of all peoples, one their origin, for God made the whole human race to live over the face of the earth.[1] One also is their final goal, God. His providence, His manifestations of goodness, His saving design extends to all men,[2] until that time when the elect will be united in the Holy City, the city ablaze with the glory of God, where the nation will walk in His light.[3]

1 Cf. Acts 17:26.
2 Cf. Wis 8:1; Acts 14:17; Rom 2:6-7; 1 Tim 2:4.
3 Cf. Apoc 21:23f.

15

Men expect from the various religions answers to the unsolved riddles of the human condition, which today, even as in former times, deeply stir the hearts of men: What is man? What is the meaning, the aim of our life? What is moral good, what sin? Whence suffering and what purpose does it serve? Which is the road to true happiness? What are death, judgment and retribution after death? What, finally, is that ultimate inexpressible mystery which encompasses our existence: whence do we come, and where are we going?

2. The different non-Christian Religions
From ancient times down to the present, there is found among various peoples a certain perception of that hidden power which hovers over the course of things and over the events of human history; at times some indeed have come to the recognition of a Supreme Being, or even of a Father. This perception and recognition penetrates their lives with a profound religious sense.

Religions, however, that are bound up with an advanced culture have struggled to answer the same questions by means of more refined concepts and a more developed language. Thus of Hinduism, men contemplate the divine mystery and express it through an inexhaustible abundance of myths and through searching philosophical enquiry. They seek freedom from the anguish of our human condition either through ascetical practices or profound meditation or a flight to God with love and trust. Again, Buddhism, in its various forms, realises the radical insufficiency of this changeable world; it teaches a way by which men, in a devout and confident spirit, may be able either to acquire the state of perfect liberation, or attain, by their own efforts or through higher help, supreme illumination. Likewise, other religions found everywhere try to counter the restlessness of the human heart, each in its own manner, by proposing 'ways', comprising teachings, rules of life, and sacred rites.

The Catholic Church rejects nothing that is true and holy in these religions. She regards with sincere reverence those ways of conduct and of life, those precepts and teachings which, though differing in many aspects from the ones she holds and sets forth, nonetheless often reflect a ray of that Truth which enlightens all men. Indeed, she proclaims, and ever must proclaim Christ, 'the way, the truth, and the life' (Jn 14:6), in whom men may find the fullness of religious life, in whom God has reconciled all things to Himself.[4]

The Church, therefore, exhorts her sons, that through dialogue and collaboration with the followers of other religions, carried out with prudence and love and in witness to the Christian faith and life, they recognise, preserve and promote the good things, spiritual and moral, as well as the socio-cultural values found among these men.

3. Islam
The Church regards with esteem also the Moslems. They adore the one God, living and subsisting in Himself, merciful and all-powerful, the Creator of heaven and earth[5] who has spoken to men; they take pains to submit wholeheartedly to even His inscrutable decrees, just as Abraham, with whom the faith of Islam takes pleasure in linking itself, submitted to God. Though they do not acknowledge Jesus as God,

4 Cf. 2 Cor 5: 18-19.
5 Cf. St Gregory VII, Letter XXI to Anzir (Nacir), king of Mauritania (PL 148, co. 450f.)

they revere Him as a prophet. They also honour Mary, his virgin mother; at times they even call on her with devotion. In addition, they await the day of judgment when God will render their deserts to all those who have been raised up from the dead. Finally, they value the moral life and worship of God especially through prayer, almsgiving and fasting.

Since in the course of centuries not a few quarrels and hostilities have arisen between Christians and Moslems, this Sacred Synod urges all to forget the past and to work sincerely for mutual understanding and to preserve as well as to promote together for the benefit of all mankind social justice and moral welfare, as well as peace and freedom.

4. Judaism

As this Sacred Synod searches into the mystery of the Church it remembers the bond that spiritually ties the people of the New Covenant to Abraham's stock.

Thus the Church of Christ acknowledges that, according to God's saving design, the beginnings of her faith and her election are found already among the Patriarchs, Moses and the Prophets. She professes that all who believe in Christ - Abraham's sons according to faith[6] - are included in the same Patriarch's call, and likewise that the salvation of the Church is mysteriously foreshadowed by the chosen people's exodus from the land of bondage. The Church, therefore, cannot forget that she received the revelation of the Old Testament through the people with whom God in His inexpressible mercy concluded the Ancient Covenant. Nor can she forget that she draws sustenance from the root of that

6 Cf. Gal 3:7.

18

well-cultivated olive tree onto which have been grafted the wild shoots, the Gentiles.[7] Indeed, the Church believes that by His cross Christ Our Peace reconciled Jews and Gentiles, making both one in Himself.[8]

The Church keeps ever in mind the words of the Apostle about his kinsmen: 'theirs is the sonship and the glory and the covenant and the law and the worship and the promises; theirs are the fathers and from them is the Christ according to the flesh' (Rom 9:4-5), the Son of the Virgin Mary. She also recalls that the Apostles, the Church's mainstay and pillars, as well as most of the early disciples who proclaimed Christ's Gospel to the world, sprang from the Jewish people.

As Holy Scripture testifies, Jerusalem did not recognise the time of her visitation,[9] nor did the Jews, in large number, accept the Gospel; indeed not a few opposed its spreading.[10] Nevertheless, God holds the Jews most dear for the sake of their Fathers; He does not repent of the gifts He makes or of the calls He issues - such is the witness of the Apostle.[11] In company with the Prophets and the same Apostle, the Church awaits that day, known to God alone, on which all peoples will address the Lord in a single voice and 'serve him shoulder to shoulder' (Soph 3:9).[12]

7 Cf. Rom 11:17-24.
8 Cf. Eph 2:14-16.
9 Cf. Lk 19:44.
10 Cf. Rom 11:28.
11 Cf. Rom 11:28-29; cf. Dogmatic Constitution *Lumen Gentium* (Light of Nations), AAS 57 (1965), p.20.
12 Cf. Is 66:23; Ps 65:4; Rom 11:11-32.

Since the spiritual patrimony common to Christians and Jews is thus so great, this Sacred Synod wants to foster and recommend that mutual understanding and respect which is the fruit, above all, of biblical and theological studies as well as of fraternal dialogues.

True, the Jewish authorities and those who followed their lead pressed for the death of Christ;[13] still, what happened in His passion cannot be charged against all the Jews, without distinction, then alive, nor against the Jews of today. Although the Church is the new people of God, the Jews should not be presented as rejected by God or accursed, as if this followed from the Holy Scriptures. All should see to it, then, that in catechetical work or in the preaching of the word of God they do not teach anything that does not conform to the truth of the Gospel and the spirit of Christ.

Furthermore, in her rejection of every persecution against any man, the Church, mindful of the patrimony she shares with the Jews and moved by the spiritual love of the Gospel and not by political reasons, decries hatred, persecutions, manifestations of anti-Semitism, directed against Jews at any time and by anyone.

Besides, as the Church has always held and holds now, Christ underwent His passion and death freely, because of the sins of men and out of infinite love, in order that all may reach salvation. It is, therefore, the burden of the Church's preaching to proclaim the cross of Christ as the sign of God's all-embracing love and as the fountain from which every grace flows.

13 Cf. Jn 19:6

5. The Brotherhood of Man

We cannot truly call on God, the Father of all, if we refuse to treat in a brotherly way any man, created as he is in the image of God. Man's relation to God the Father and his relation to men his brothers are so linked together that Scripture says: 'He who does not love does not know God' (1 Jn 4:8).

No foundation therefore remains for any theory or practice that leads to discrimination between man and man or people and people, so far as their human dignity and the rights flowing from it are concerned.

The Church reproves, as foreign to the mind of Christ, any discrimination against men or harassment of them because of their race, colour, condition in life, or religion. On the contrary, following in the footsteps of the holy Apostles Peter and Paul, this Sacred Synod ardently implores the Christian faithful to maintain good fellowship among the nations (1 Pet 2:12), and, if possible, to live for their part in peace with all men, [14] so that they may truly be sons of the Father who is in heaven. (15 Cf. Mt 5:45)

14 Cf. Rom 12:18.

2. GUIDELINES AND SUGGESTIONS FOR IMPLEMENTING THE CONCILIAR DECLARATION NOSTRA AETATE (NO. 4) (DECEMBER 1, 1974)

VATICAN COMMISSION FOR RELIGIOUS RELATIONS WITH THE JEWS

Preamble

The Declaration *Nostra Aetate*, issued by the Second Vatican Council on 28 October 1965, "on the relationship of the Church to non-Christian religions" (no. 4) marks an important milestone in the history of Jewish-Christian relations.

Moreover, the step taken by the council finds its historical setting in circumstances deeply affected by the memory of the persecution and massacre of Jews which took place in Europe just before and during the Second World War.

Although Christianity sprang from Judaism, taking from it certain essential elements of faith and divine cult, the gap dividing them was deepened more and more, to such an extent that Christian and Jew hardly knew each other.

After two thousand years, too often marked by mutual ignorance and frequent confrontation, the Declaration *Nostra Aetate* provides an opportunity to open or to continue a dialogue with a view to better mutual understanding. Over the past nine years, many steps in this direction have been taken in various countries. As a result, it is easier to distinguish the conditions under which a new relationship between Jews and Christians may be worked out and developed. This seems the right moment to propose, following the guidelines of the council, some concrete suggestions born of experience, hoping that they will help to bring into actual existence in the life of the Church the intentions expressed in the conciliar document.

While referring the reader back to this document, we may simply restate here that the spiritual bonds and historical links binding the Church to Judaism, condemn (as opposed to the very spirit of Christianity) all forms of anti-Semitism and discrimination, which in any case the dignity of the human person alone would suffice to condemn. Further still, these links and relationships render obligatory a better mutual understanding and renewed mutual esteem. On the practical level in particular, Christians must therefore strive to acquire a better knowledge of the basic components of the religious tradition of Judaism; they must strive to learn by what essential traits the Jews define themselves in the light of their own religious experience.

With due respect for such matters of principle, we simply propose some first practical applications in different essential areas of the Church's life, with a view to launching or developing sound relations between Catholics and their Jewish brothers.

I. Dialogue
To tell the truth, such relations as there have been between Jew and Christian have scarcely ever risen above the level of monologue. From now on, real discourse must be established.

Dialogue presupposes that each side wishes to know the other, and wishes to increase and deepen its knowledge of the other. It constitutes a particularly suitable means of favouring a better mutual knowledge and, especially in the case of dialogue between Jews and Christians, of probing the riches of one's own tradition. Dialogue demands respect for the other as he is; above all respect for his faith and his religious convictions.

In virtue of her divine mission, and her very nature, the Church must preach Jesus Christ to the world (*Ad Gentes*, 2). Lest the witness of Catholics to Jesus Christ should give offence to Jews, they must take care to live and spread their Christian faith while maintaining the strictest respect for religious liberty in line with the teaching of the Second Vatican Council (Declaration *Dignitatis Humanae*). They will likewise strive to understand the difficulties which arise for the Jewish soul - rightly imbued with an extremely high, pure notion of the divine transcendence - when faced with the mystery of the incarnate Word.

While it is true that a widespread air of suspicion, inspired by an unfortunate past, is still dominant in this particular area, Christians, for their part, will be able to see to what extent the responsibility is theirs and deduce practical conclusions for the future.

In addition to friendly talks, competent people will be encouraged to meet and to study together the many problems deriving from the fundamental convictions of Judaism and of Christianity. In order not to hurt (even involuntarily) those taking part, it will be vital to guarantee, not only tact, but a great openness of spirit and diffidence with respect to one's own prejudices.

In whatever circumstances as shall prove possible and mutually acceptable, one might encourage a common meeting in the presence of God, in prayer and silent meditation, a highly efficacious way of finding that humility, that openness of heart and mind, necessary prerequisites for a deep knowledge of oneself and of others. In particular, that will be done in connection with great causes such as the struggle for peace and justice.

II. Liturgy

The existing links between the Christian liturgy and the Jewish liturgy will be borne in mind. The idea of a living community in the service of God, and in the service of men for the love of God, such as it is realised in the liturgy, is just as characteristic of the Jewish liturgy as it is of the Christian one. To improve Jewish-Christian relations, it is important to take cognizance of those common elements of the liturgical life (formulas, feasts, rites, etc.) in which the Bible holds an essential place.

An effort will be made to acquire a better understanding of whatever in the Old Testament retains its own perpetual value (cf. *Dei Verbum*, 14-15), since that has not been cancelled by the later interpretation of the New Testament. Rather, the New Testament brings out the full meaning of the Old, while both Old and New illumine and explain each other (cf. *ibid.*, 16). This is all the more important since liturgical reform is now bringing the text of the Old Testament ever more frequently to the attention of Christians.

When commenting on biblical texts, emphasis will be laid on the continuity of our faith with that of the earlier Covenant, in the perspective of the promises, without minimising those elements of Christianity which are original. We believe that those promises were fulfilled with the first coming of Christ. But it is nonetheless true that we still await their perfect fulfilment in his glorious return at the end of time.

With respect to liturgical readings, care will be taken to see that homilies based on them will not distort their meaning, especially when it is a question of passages which seem to show the Jewish people as such in an unfavourable light. Efforts will be made so to instruct the Christian people that they will understand the true interpretation of all the texts and their meaning for the contemporary believer.

Commissions entrusted with the task of liturgical translation will pay particular attention to the way in which they express those phrases and passages which Christians, if not well informed, might misunderstand because of prejudice. Obviously, one cannot alter the text of the Bible. The point is that, with a version destined for liturgical use, there should be an overriding preoccupation to bring out explicitly the meaning of a text.[1]

1 Thus the formula "the Jews", in St John, sometimes according to the context means "the leaders of the Jews", or "the adversaries of Jesus", terms which express better the thought of the evangelist and avoid appearing to arraign the Jewish people as such. Another example is the use of the words "Pharisee" and "Pharisaism" which have taken on a largely pejorative meaning) while taking scriptural studies into account.

The preceding remarks also apply to introductions to biblical readings, to the Prayer of the Faithful, and to commentaries printed in missals used by the laity.

III. Teaching and Education

Although there is still a great deal of work to be done, a better understanding of Judaism itself and its relationship to Christianity has been achieved in recent years thanks to the teaching of the Church, the study and research of scholars, as also to the beginning of dialogue.

In this respect, the following facts deserve to be recalled:

◆ It is the same God, "inspirer and author of the books of both Testaments" (*Dei Verbum*, 16), who speaks both in the old and new Covenants.

◆ Judaism in the time of Christ and the Apostles was a complex reality, embracing many different trends, many spiritual, religious, social and cultural values.

◆ The Old Testament and the Jewish tradition founded upon it must not be set against the New Testament in such a way that the former seems to constitute a religion of only justice, fear and legalism, with no appeal to the love of God and neighbour (cf. Dt 6:5; Lv 19:18; Mt 22:34-40).

◆ Jesus was born of the Jewish people, as were his Apostles and a large number of his first disciples. When he revealed himself as the Messiah and Son of God (cf. Mt 16:16), the bearer of the new gospel message, he did so as the fulfilment and perfection of the earlier Revelation. And, although his teaching had a profoundly new character, Christ, nevertheless, in many instances, took his stand on the teaching of the Old Testament. The New Testament is profoundly marked by its relation to the Old. As the Second

27

Vatican Council declared: "God, the inspirer and author of the books of both Testaments, wisely arranged that the New Testament be hidden in the Old and the Old be made manifest in the New" (*Dei Verbum*, 16). Jesus also used teaching methods similar to those employed by the rabbis of his time.

◆ With regard to the trial and death of Jesus, the Council recalled that "what happened in his passion cannot be blamed upon all the Jews then living, without distinction, nor upon the Jews of today" (*Nostra Aetate*, 4).

◆ The history of Judaism did not end with the destruction of Jerusalem, but rather went on to develop a religious tradition. And, although we believe that the importance and meaning of that tradition were deeply affected by the coming of Christ, it is still nonetheless rich in religious values.

◆ With the prophets and the apostle Paul, "the Church awaits the day, known to God alone, on which all peoples will address the Lord in a single voice and 'serve Him with one accord' (Soph 3:9)" (*Nostra Aetate*, 4).

Information concerning these questions is important at all levels of Christian instruction and education. Among sources of information, special attention should be paid to the following:

◆ catechism and religious textbooks;

◆ history books;

◆ the mass-media (press, radio, cinema, television).

The effective use of these means presupposes the thorough formation of instructors and educators in training schools, seminaries and universities.

Research into the problems bearing on Judaism and Jewish-Christian relations will be encouraged among specialists, particularly in the fields of exegesis, theology, history and sociology. Higher institutions of Catholic research, in association if possible with other similar Christian institutions and experts, are invited to contribute to the solution of such problems. Wherever possible, chairs of Jewish studies will be created, and collaboration with Jewish scholars encouraged.

IV. Joint Social Action

Jewish and Christian tradition, founded on the Word of God, is aware of the value of the human person, the image of God. Love of the same God must show itself in effective action for the good of mankind. In the spirit of the prophets, Jews and Christians will work willingly together, seeking social justice and peace at every level - local, national and international.

At the same time, such collaboration can do much to foster mutual understanding and esteem.

Conclusion

The Second Vatican Council has pointed out the path to follow in promoting deep fellowship between Jews and Christians. But there is still a long road ahead.

The problem of Jewish-Christian relations concerns the Church as such, since it is when "pondering her own mystery" that she encounters the mystery of Israel. Therefore, even in areas where no Jewish communities exist, this remains an important problem. There is also an ecumenical aspect to the question: the very return of Christians to the sources and origins of their faith, grafted on to the earlier Covenant, helps the search for unity in Christ, the cornerstone.

In this field, the bishops will know what best to do on the pastoral level, within the general disciplinary framework of the Church and in line with the common teaching of her magisterium. For example, they will create some suitable commissions or secretariats on a national or regional level, or appoint some competent person to promote the implementation of the conciliar directives and the suggestions made above.

On 22 October 1974, the Holy Father instituted for the universal Church this Commission for Religious Relations with the Jews, joined to the Secretariat for Promoting Christian Unity. This special Commission, created to encourage and foster religious relations between Jews and Catholics - and to do so eventually in collaboration with other Christians - will be, within the limits of its competence, at the service of all interested organisations, providing information for them, and helping them to pursue their task in conformity .with the instructions of the Holy See.

The Commission wishes to develop this collaboration in order to implement, correctly and effectively, the express intentions of the council.

Given at Rome, 1 December 1974.

✚ Johannes Cardinal Willebrands
President of the Commission

Pierre-Marie de Contenson, OP
Secretary of the Commission

3. Notes on the Correct Way to Present the Jews and Judaism in Preaching and Catechesis in the Roman Catholic Church (June 24, 1985)

Vatican Commission for Religious Relations with the Jews

Preliminary Considerations

On March 6, 1982, Pope John Paul II told delegates of episcopal conferences and other experts, meeting in Rome to study relations between the church and Judaism: "...you yourselves were concerned during your sessions, with Catholic teaching and catechesis regarding Jews and Judaism... We should aim, in this field, that Catholic teaching at its different levels, in catechesis to children and young people, presents Jews and Judaism, not only in an honest and objective manner, free from prejudices and without any offences, but also with full awareness of the heritage common to Jews and Christians".

In this passage, so charged with meaning, the Holy Father plainly drew inspiration from the Council Declaration *Nostra Aetate*, 4, which says:

"All should take pains, then, lest in catechetical instruction and in the preaching of God's Word they teach anything out of harmony with the truth of the gospel and the spirit of Christ"; as also from these words: "Since the spiritual patrimony common to Christians and Jews is thus so great, this sacred Synod wishes to foster and recommend mutual understanding and respect..."

In the same way, the *Guidelines and Suggestions* for implementing the Conciliar declaration *Nostra Aetate* (no. 4) ends its chapter III, entitled "Teaching and education", which lists a number of practical things to be done, with this recommendation: "Information concerning these questions is important at all levels of Christian instruction and education. Among sources of information, special attention should be paid to the following:

◆ catechisms and religious textbooks;

◆ history books;

◆ the mass media (press, radio, cinema, television).

The effective use of these means presupposes the thorough formation of instructors and educators in training schools, seminaries and universities" (AAS 77 (1975) 73).

The paragraphs which follow are intended to serve this purpose.

I. Religious Teaching and Judaism

1. In *Nostra Aetate* 4, the Council speaks of the "spiritual bonds linking" Jews and Christians and of the "great spiritual patrimony" common to both and it further asserts that "the Church of Christ acknowledges that, according to the mystery of God's saving design, the beginning of her faith and her election are already found among the patriarchs, Moses and the prophets".

2. Because of the unique relations that exist between Christianity and Judaism - "linked together at the very level of their identity" (John Paul II, 6 March 1982) - relations "founded on the design of the God of the Covenant" (*ibid.*), the Jews and Judaism should not occupy an occasional and marginal place in catech-

esis: their presence there is essential and should be organically integrated.

3. This concern for Judaism in Catholic teaching has not merely a historical or archeological foundation. As the Holy Father said in the speech already quoted, after he had again mentioned the "common patrimony" of the Church and Judaism as "considerable": "To assess it carefully in itself and with due awareness of the faith and religious life of the Jewish people *as they are professed and practiced still today*, can greatly help us to understand better certain aspects of the life of the Church" (italics added). It is a question then of *pastoral* concern for a still living reality closely related to the Church. The Holy Father has stated this permanent reality of the Jewish people in a remarkable theological formula, in his allocution to the Jewish community of West Germany at Mainz, on November 17, 1980: "... the people of God of the Old Covenant, which has never been revoked..."

4. Here we should recall the passage in which the *Guidelines and Suggestions*, I, tried to define the fundamental condition of dialogue: "respect for the other as he is", knowledge of the "basic components of the religious tradition of Judaism" and again learning "by what essential traits the Jews define themselves in the light of their own religious experience" (*Introd.*).

5. The singular character and the difficulty of Christian teaching about Jews and Judaism lies in this, that it needs to balance a number of pairs of ideas which express the relation between the two economies of the Old and New Testaments:

Promise and Fulfilment

Continuity and Newness

33

Singularity and Universality
Uniqueness and Exemplary Nature.

This means that the theologian and the catechist who deals with the subject needs to show in his practice of teaching that:

◆ promise and fulfilment throw light on each other;
◆ newness lies in a metamorphosis of what was there before;
◆ the singularity of the people of the Old Testament is not exclusive and is open, in the divine vision, to a universal extension;
◆ the uniqueness of the Jewish people is meant to have the force of an example.

6. Finally, "work that is of poor quality and lacking in precision would be extremely detrimental" to Judaeo-Christian dialogue (John Paul II, speech of March 6, 1982). But it would be above all detrimental - since we are talking of teaching and education - to Christian identity (*ibid.*).

7. "In virtue of her divine mission, the Church" which is to be "the all-embracing means of salvation" in which alone "the fullness of the means of salvation can be obtained" (*Unitatis Redintegratio*, 3), "must of her nature proclaim Jesus Christ to the world" (cf. *Guidelines and Suggestions*, I). Indeed we believe that it is through Him that we go to the Father (cf. Jn 14:6) "and this is eternal life, that they know You the only true God and Jesus Christ whom You have sent" (Jn 17:3).

Jesus affirms (*ibid.* 10:16) that "there shall be one flock and one shepherd". Church and Judaism cannot then be seen as two parallel ways of salvation and the

Church must witness to Christ as the Redeemer for all, "while maintaining the strictest respect for religious liberty in line with the teaching of the Second Vatican Council (Declaration *Dignitatis Humanae*" *(Guidelines and Suggestions, I)*.

8. The urgency and importance of precise, objective and rigorously accurate teaching on Judaism for our faithful follows too from the danger of anti-Semitism which is always ready to reappear under different guises. The question is not merely to uproot from among the faithful the remains of anti-Semitism still to be found here and there, but much rather to arouse in them, through educational work, an exact knowledge of the wholly unique "bond" *(Nostra Aetate*, 4) which joins us as a Church to the Jews and to Judaism. In this way, they would learn to appreciate and love the latter, who have been chosen by God to prepare the coming of Christ and have preserved everything that was progressively revealed and given in the course of that preparation, notwithstanding their difficulty in recognising in Him their Messiah.

II. Relations between the Old[1] and New Testament

1. Our aim should be to show the unity of Biblical Revelation (O.T. and N.T.) and of the divine plan, before speaking of each historical event, so as to stress that particular events have meaning when seen in history as whole - from creation to fulfilment. Thus the definitive meaning of the election of Israel does not become clear except in the light of the complete fulfil-

1 We continue to use the expression Old Testament because it is traditional (cf. already 2 Co 3:14) but also because "Old" does not mean "out of date" or "outworn". In any case, it is the permanent value of the O.T. as a source of Christian Revelation that is emphasised here (cf. *Dei Verbum*, 3).

ment (Rm 9-11) and election in Jesus Christ is still better understood with reference to the announcement and the promise (cf. Heb 4:1-11).

2. We are dealing with singular happenings which concern a singular nation but are destined, in the sight of God who reveals His purpose, to take on universal and exemplary significance.

The aim is moreover to present the events of the Old Testament not as concerning only the Jews but also as touching us personally. Abraham is truly the father of our faith (cf. Rm 4:11-12; Roman Canon: *patriarchae nostri Abrahae*). And it is said (1 Co 10:1): "Our fathers were all under the cloud, and all passed through the sea". The patriarchs, prophets and other personalities of the Old Testament have been venerated and always will be venerated as saints in the liturgical tradition of the Oriental Church as also of the Latin Church.

3. From the unity of the divine plan derives the problem of the relation between the Old and New Testaments. The Church already from apostolic times (cf. 1 Co 10:11; Heb 10:1) and then constantly in tradition resolved this problem by means of typology, which emphasises the primordial value that the Old Testament must have in the Christian view. Typology, however, makes many people uneasy and is perhaps a sign of a problem unresolved.

4. Hence, in using typology, the teaching and practice which we have received from the Liturgy and from the Fathers of the Church, we should be careful to avoid any transition from the Old to the New Testament

which might seem merely a rupture. The Church, in the spontaneity of the Spirit which animates her, has vigorously condemned the attitude of Marcion[2] and always opposed his dualism.

5. It should also be emphasised that typological interpretation consists in reading the Old Testament as preparation and, in certain aspects, outline and foreshadowing of the New (cf., e.g. Heb 5:5-10, etc.). Christ is henceforth the key and point of reference to the Scriptures: "the rock was Christ" (1 Co 10:4).

6. It is true then, and should be stressed, that the Church and Christians read the Old Testament in the light of the event of the dead and risen Christ and that on these grounds there is a Christian reading of the Old Testament which does not necessarily coincide with the Jewish reading. Thus Christian identity and Jewish identity should be carefully distinguished in their respective reading of the Bible. But this detracts nothing from the value of the Old Testament in the Church and does nothing to hinder Christians from profiting discerningly from the traditions of Jewish reading.

7. Typological reading only manifests the unfathomable riches of the Old Testament, its inexhaustible content and the mystery of which it is full, and should not lead us to forget that it retains its own value as Revelation that the New Testament often does no more than resume (cf. Mk 12:29-31). Moreover, the New

2 A man of gnostic tendency who in the second century rejected the Old Testament and part of the New as the work of an evil god, a demiurge. The Church reacted strongly against this heresy (cf. Irenaeus)

Testament itself demands to be read in the light of the Old. Primitive Christian catechesis constantly had recourse to this (cf., e.g. 1 Co 5:6-8; 10:1-11).

8. Typology further signifies reaching towards the accomplishment of the divine plan, when "God will be all in all" (1 Cor 15:28). This holds true also for the Church which, realised already in Christ, yet awaits it definitive perfecting as the Body of Christ. The fact that the Body of Christ is still tending towards its full stature (cf. Ep 4:12-19) takes nothing from the value of being a Christian. So also the calling of the patriarchs and the Exodus from Egypt do not lose their importance and value in God's design from being at the same time intermediate stages (cf., e.g. *Nostra Aetate*, 4).

9. The Exodus, for example, represents an experience of salvation and liberation that is not complete in itself, but has in it, over and above its own meaning, the capacity to be developed further. Salvation and liberation are already accomplished in Christ and gradually realised by the sacraments in the Church. This makes way for the fulfilment of God's design, which awaits its final consummation with the return of Jesus as Messiah, for which we pray each day. The Kingdom, for the coming of which we also pray each day, will be finally established. With salvation and liberation the elect and the whole of Creation will be transformed in Christ (Rm 8:19-23).

10. Furthermore, in underlining the eschatological dimension of Christianity we shall reach a greater awareness that the people of God of the Old and the New Testament are tending towards a like end in the

future: the coming or return of the Messiah - even if they start from two different points of view. It is more clearly understood that the person of the Messiah is not only a point of division for the people of God but also a point of convergence (cf. *Sussidi per l'ecumenismo* of the diocese of Rome, n. 140). Thus it can be said that Jews and Christians meet in a comparable hope, founded on the same promise made to Abraham (cf. Gn 12:1-3; Heb 6:13-18).

11. Attentive to the same God who has spoken, hanging on the same word, we have to witness to one same memory and one common hope in Him who is the master of history. We must also accept our responsibility to prepare the world for the coming of the Messiah by working together for social justice, respect for the rights of persons and nations and for social and international reconciliation. To this we are driven, Jews and Christians, by the command to love our neighbour, by a common hope for the Kingdom of God and by the great heritage of the Prophets. Transmitted soon enough by catechesis, such a conception would teach young Christians in a practical way to co-operate with Jews, going beyond simple dialogue (cf. *Guidelines*, IV).

III. Jewish Roots of Christianity

12. Jesus was and always remained a Jew, his ministry was deliberately limited "to the lost sheep of the house of Israel" (Mt 15:24). Jesus is fully a man of his time, and of his environment - the Jewish Palestinian one of the first century, the anxieties and hopes of which he shared. This cannot but underline both the reality of the Incarnation and the very meaning of the history of salvation, as it has been revealed in the Bible (cf. Rm 1:34; Ga 4:4-5).

13. Jesus' relations with biblical law and its more or less traditional interpretations are undoubtedly complex and he showed great liberty towards it (cf. the "antitheses" of the Sermon on the Mount: Mt 5:21-48, bearing in mind the exegetical difficulties; his attitude to rigorous observance of the Sabbath: Mk 3:1-6, etc.).

But there is no doubt that he wished to submit himself to the law (cf. Ga 4:4), that he was circumcised and presented in the Temple like any Jew of his time (cf. Lk 2:21, 22-24), that he was trained in the law's observance. He extolled respect for it (cf. Mt 5:17-20) and invited obedience to it (cf. Mt 8:4). The rhythm of his life was marked by observance of pilgrimages on great feasts, even from his infancy (cf. Lk 2:41-50; Jn 2:13; 7-10, etc.). The importance of the cycle of the Jewish feasts has been frequently underlined in the Gospel of John (cf. 2:13; 5:1; 7:2.10.37; 10:22; 12:1; 13:1; 18:28; 19:42, etc.).

14. It should be noted also that Jesus often taught in the Synagogues (cf. Mt 4:23; 9:35; Lk 4:15-18; Jn 18:20, etc.) and in the Temple (cf. Jn 18:20, etc.), which he frequented as did the disciples even after the Resurrection (cf. e.g. Ac 2:46; 3:1; 21:26, etc.). He wished to put in the context of synagogue worship the proclamation of his Messiahship (cf. Lk 4:16-21). But above all he wished to achieve the supreme act of the gift of himself in the setting of the domestic liturgy of the Passover, or at least of the paschal festivity (cf. Mk 14:1.12 and parallels; Jn 18:28). This also allows of a better understanding of the "memorial" character of the Eucharist.

15. Thus the Son of God is incarnate in a people and a human family (cf. Ga 4:4; Rm 9:5). This takes away nothing, quite the contrary, from the fact that he was born for all men (Jewish shepherds and pagan wise men are found at his crib: Lk 2:8-20; Mt 2:1-12) and died for all men (at the foot of the cross there are Jews, among them Mary and John: Jn 19:25-27, and pagans like the Centurion: Mk 15:39 and parallels). Thus he made two peoples one in his flesh (cf. Ep 2:14-17). This explains why with the *Ecclesia ex gentibus* we have, in Palestine and elsewhere, an *Ecclesia ex circumcisione*, of which Eusebius for example speaks (H.E., IV, 5).

16. His relations with the Pharisees were not always or wholly polemical. Of this there are many proofs:

◆ It is Pharisees who warn Jesus of the risks he is running (Lk 13:31);
◆ Some Pharisees are praised - e.g. "the scribe" of Mk 12:34;
◆ Jesus eats with Pharisees (Lk 7:36; 14:1).

17. Jesus shares, with the majority of Palestinian Jews of that time, some pharisaic doctrines: the resurrection of the body; forms of piety, like alms-giving, prayer, fasting (cf. Mt 6:1-18) and the liturgical practice of addressing God as Father; the priority of the commandment to love God and our neighbour (cf. Mk 12:28-34). This is so also with Paul (cf. Ac 23:8), who always considered his membership of the Pharisees as a title of honour (cf. *ibid.*, 23:6; 26:5; Ph 3:5).

18. Paul also, like Jesus himself, used methods of reading and interpreting Scripture and of teaching his

disciples which were common to the Pharisees of their time. This applies to the use of parables in Jesus' ministry, as also to the method of Jesus and Paul of supporting a conclusion with a quotation from Scripture.

19. It is noteworthy too that the Pharisees are not mentioned in accounts of the Passion. Gamaliel (Ac 5:34-39) defends the apostles in a meeting of the Sanhedrin. An exclusively negative picture of the Pharisees is likely to be inaccurate and unjust (cf. *Guidelines*, Note 1; cf. AAS, p. 76). If in the Gospel and elsewhere in the New Testament there are all sorts of unfavourable references to the Pharisees, they should be seen against the background of a complex and diversified movement. Criticisms of various types of Pharisees are moreover not lacking in rabbinical sources (cf. the *Babylonian Talmud*, the *Sotah* treatise 22b, etc.). "Phariseeism" in the pejorative sense can be rife in any religion. It may also be stressed that, if Jesus shows himself severe towards the Pharisees, it is because he is closer to them than to other contemporary Jewish groups (cf. *supra* no. 17).

20. All this should help us to understand better what St Paul says (Rm 11:16 ff) about the "root" and the "branches". The Church and Christianity, for all their novelty, find their origin in the Jewish milieu of the first century of our era, and more deeply still in the "design of God" (*Nostra Aetate*, 4), realised in the Patriarchs, Moses and the Prophets (*ibid.*), down to its consummation in Christ Jesus.

IV. The Jews in the New Testament

21. The *Guidelines* already say (note 1) that "the formula 'the Jews' sometimes, according to the context, means 'the leaders of the Jews' or 'the adversaries of

Jesus', terms which express better the thought of the evangelist and avoid appearing to arraign the Jewish people as such".

An objective presentation of the role of the Jewish people in the New Testament should take account of these various facts:

(A) The Gospels are the outcome of long and complicated editorial work. The dogmatic constitution *Dei Verbum*, following the Pontifical Biblical Commission's Instruction *Sancta Mater Ecclesia*, distinguished three stages: "The sacred authors wrote the four Gospels, selecting some things from the many which had been handed on by word of mouth or in writing, reducing some of them to a synthesis, explicating some things in view of the situation of their Churches, and preserving the form of proclamation, but always in such fashion that they told us the honest truth about Jesus" (no. 19).

Hence it cannot be ruled out that some references hostile or less than favourable to the Jews have their historical context in conflicts between the ancient Church and the Jewish community. Certain controversies reflect Christian-Jewish relations long after the time of Jesus.

To establish this is of capital importance if we wish to bring out the meaning of certain Gospel texts for the Christians of today.

All this should be taken into account when preparing catechesis and homilies for the last weeks of Lent and Holy Week (cf. already *Guidelines* II, and now also *Sussidi per l'ecumenismo nella diocesi di Roma,* 1982, 144b).

(B) It is clear on the other hand that there were conflicts between Jesus and certain categories of Jews of his time, among them Pharisees from the beginning of his ministry (cf. Mk 2:1-11.24; 3:6, etc.).

(C) There is moreover the sad fact that the majority of the Jewish people and its authorities did not believe in Jesus - a fact not merely of history but of theological bearing, of which St Paul tries hard to plumb the meaning (Rm chap. 9-11).

(D) This fact, accentuated as the Christian mission developed, especially among the pagans, led inevitably to a rupture between Judaism and the young Church, now irreducibly separated and divergent in faith, and this stage of affairs is reflected in the texts of the New Testament and particularly in the Gospels. There is no question of playing down or glossing over this rupture; that could only prejudice the identity of either side. Nevertheless it certainly does not cancel the spiritual "bond" of which the Council speaks (*Nostra Aetate*, 4) and which we propose to dwell on here.

(E) Reflecting on this in the light of Scripture, notably of the chapters cited from the Epistle to the Romans, Christians should never forget that the faith is a free gift of God (cf. Rm 9:12) and that we should never judge the consciences of others. St Paul's exhortation "do not boast" in your attitude to "the root" (Rm 11:18) has its full point here.

(F) There is no putting the Jews who knew Jesus and did not believe in him, or those who opposed the preaching of the apostles, on the same plane with Jews who came after or those of today. If the responsibility of the former remains a mystery hidden with God (cf. Rm 11:25), the latter are in an entirely different situation. Vatican II in the declaration on *Religious Liberty* teaches that "all men are to be immune from coercion... in such wise that in matters religious no one is to be forced to act in a manner contrary to his own beliefs. Nor... restrained from acting in accordance with his own beliefs" (no. 2). This is one of the bases - proclaimed by the Council - on which Judaeo-Christian dialogue rests.

22. The delicate question of responsibility for the death of Christ must be looked at from the standpoint of the conciliar declaration *Nostra Aetate*, 4 and of *Guidelines and Suggestions* (§ III): "What happened in (Christ's) passion cannot be blamed upon all the Jews then living without distinction nor upon the Jews of today", especially since "authorities of the Jews and those who followed their lead pressed for the death of Christ". Again, further on: "Christ in his boundless love freely underwent his passion and death because of the sins of all men, so that all might attain salvation" (*Nostra Aetate*, 4). The Catechism of the Council of Trent teaches that Christian sinners are more to blame for the death of Christ than those few Jews who brought it about - they indeed "knew not what they did" (cf. Lk 23:34) and we know it only too well (Pars I, caput V, Quaest. XI). In the same way and for the same reason, "the Jews should not be presented as repudiated or cursed by God, as if such views followed from the holy Scriptures" (*Nostra Aetate*, 4), even though it is true that "the Church is the new people of God" (*ibid.*).

45

V. The Liturgy

23. Jews and Christians find in the Bible the very substance of their liturgy: for the proclamation of God's word, response to it, prayer of praise and intercession for the living and the dead, recourse to the divine mercy. The Liturgy of the word in its own structure originates in Judaism. The prayer of Hours and other liturgical texts and formularies have their parallels in Judaism as do the very formulas of our most venerable prayers, among them the Our Father. The Eucharistic prayers also draw inspiration from models in the Jewish tradition. As John Paul II said (Allocution of March 6, 1982): "... the faith and religious life of the Jewish people as they are professed and practiced still today, can greatly help us to understand better certain aspects of the life of the Church. Such is the case of liturgy..."

24. This is particularly evident in the great feasts of the liturgical years, like the Passover. Christians and Jews celebrate the Passover: the Jews, the historic Passover looking towards the future; the Christians, the Passover accomplished in the death and resurrection of Christ, although still in expectation of the final consummation (cf. *supra* no. 9). It is still the "memorial" which comes to us from the Jewish tradition, with a specific content different in each case. On either side, however, there is a like dynamism: for Christians it gives meaning to the Eucharistic celebration (cf. the antiphon *O sacrum convivium*), a paschal celebration and as such a making present of the past, but experienced in the expectation of what is to come.

VI. Judaism and Christianity in History

25. The history of Israel did not end in 70 A.D. (cf. *Guidelines*, II). It continued, especially in a numerous

46

Diaspora which allowed Israel to carry to the whole world a witness - often heroic - of its fidelity to the one God and to "exalt Him in the presence of all the living" (Tobit 13:4), while preserving the memory of the land of their forefathers at the heart of their hope (Passover *Seder*).

Christians are invited to understand this religious attachment which finds its root in Biblical tradition, without however making their own any particular religious interpretation of this relationship (cf. Declaration of the U.S. Conference of Catholic Bishops, November 20, 1975).

The existence of the State of Israel and its political options should be envisaged not in a perspective which is in itself religious, but in their reference to the common principles of international law.

The permanence of Israel (while so many ancient peoples have disappeared without trace) is a historic fact and a sign to be interpreted within God's design. We must in any case rid ourselves of the traditional idea of a people punished, preserved as a living argument for Christian apologetic. It remains a chosen people, "the pure olive on which were grafted the branches of the wild olive which are the gentiles" (John Paul II, 6 March 1982, alluding to Rm 11:17-24). We must remember how much the balance of relations between Jews and Christians over two thousand years has been negative. We must remind ourselves how much the permanence of Israel is accompanied by a continuous spiritual fecundity, in the rabbinical period, in the Middle Ages and in modern times, taking its start from a patrimony which we long shared, so much so that "the faith

47

and religious life of the Jewish people as they are professed and practiced still today, can greatly help us to understand better certain aspects of the life of the Church" (John Paul II, March 6, 1982). Catechesis should on the other hand help in understanding the meaning for the Jews of the extermination during the years 1939-1945, and its consequences.

26. Education and catechesis should concern themselves with the problem of racism, still active in different forms of anti-Semitism. The Council presented it thus: "Moreover, (the Church) mindful of her common patrimony with the Jews and motivated by the Gospel's spiritual love and by no political considerations, deplores the hatred, persecutions and displays of anti-Semitism directed against the Jews at any time and from any source" (*Nostra Aetate*, 4). The Guidelines comment "The spiritual bonds and historical links binding the Church to Judaism condemn (as opposed to the very spirit of Christianity) all forms of anti-Semitism and discrimination, which in any case the dignity of the human person alone would suffice to condemn" (*Guidelines*, Preamble).

Conclusion

27. Religious teaching, catechesis and preaching should be a preparation not only for objectivity, justice, tolerance but also for understanding and dialogue. Our two traditions are so related that they cannot ignore each other. Mutual knowledge must be encouraged at every level. There is evident in particular a painful ignorance of the history and traditions of Judaism, of which only negative aspects and often caricature seem to form part of the stock ideas of many Christians.

That is what these notes aim to remedy. This would mean that the Council text and *Guidelines and Suggestions* would be more easily and faithfully put into practice.

✝ Johannes Cardinal Willebrands
President

Pierre Duprey
Vice-President

Jorge Mejía
Secretary

A Note for the Presentation of the Document of the Commission for Religious Relations with the Jews

(Notes on the Correct Way to Present the Jews and Judaism in Preaching and Catechesis in the Roman Catholic Church)

Jorge Mejía

The document published here is the result of long and considered work by our Commission.

At the beginning of March 1982, delegates of episcopal conferences and other experts met in Rome to examine a first daft. It was in the course of preparations for this meeting that requests from various quarters came to the Commission, asking that a guide be prepared. Such a guide would be for the use of all those in the Church who have the difficult task of presenting Jews and Judaism to the Catholic faithful in the light of new pastoral and doctrinal developments. These developments flow from the conciliar Declaration *Nostra Aetate*, 4, published twenty years ago and from the *Guidelines and Suggestions for Implementing the Conciliar Declaration "Nostra Aetate"* (no. 4), published by our Commission at the end of 1974.

The idea was to be of help to those engaged in catechetical work, in teaching and also in preaching, and to put into practice the new directions just mentioned, which are not always easy to translate into teaching methods.

The preparatory work went on for three years. There were several consultations with our consultors in Rome and elsewhere, resulting in several subsequent drafts. Clearly, throughout these stages of the work, and above all in the final one, the drafters kept well in mind what the Holy Father has had to say on Jewish-Catholic relations. He has addressed this subject on various important occasions, from Paris to Mainz, from Brooklyn to Caracas and Madrid, and many times in Rome itself. Neither could the drafters forget the various documents published in recent years by several episcopal conferences. And, at the same time, the Commission along with these consultors and experts took into account the accumulated experience of many years of nearly daily contact with our Jewish partners. For all of that, the text is and remains a document of the Catholic Church. This means that its language, its structure, and the questions it intends to address belong to the teaching and pastoral practice of the Catholic Church.

As is normal procedure with any document published by a department of the Holy See, other departments with competency in the subject matter were consulted. Their observations have been dutifully and carefully taken into account. It is both our duty and our pleasure to express our gratitude and appreciation publicly to them for their patient and fruitful collaboration with us.

The document, in this its final version, bears the title *Notes on the Correct Way to Present the Jews and Judaism in Preaching and Catechesis in the Roman Catholic Church.* The first word of the title (*Notes*) appropriately indicates the aim of the text. It is intended

51

to provide a helpful frame of reference for those who are called upon in various ways in the course of their teaching assignments to speak about Jews and Judaism and who wish to do so in keeping with the current teaching of the Church in this area. As everyone knows, this happens quite often. In fact, it is a practical impossibility to present Christianity while abstracting from the Jews and Judaism, unless one were to suppress the Old Testament, forget about the Jewishness of Jesus and the Apostles, and dismiss the vital cultural and religious context of the primitive Church. Neither is it an alterative to present one and the other in a prejudiced, unfavourable light. It is precisely this way of acting that the Council wanted to put an end to. That was also the aim that the 1974 *Guidelines* addressed more or less on the level of general principles. It is exactly the same aim that the present *Notes* address on a more concrete level - one might almost say in handbook style, as long as one keeps in mind the limitations of a text that cannot and should not be too lengthy.

Hence, the *structure* of the document. It starts with a series of "Preliminary Considerations", which introduce the spirit and the rationale of the text, mostly with the help of quotations from the Council, the Holy Father, or from preceding documents. Thereupon follows a first section called "Religious Teaching and Judaism", in which the doctrinal and pastoral principles underlying such teaching are set forth. Of special note is paragraph no. 3, which speaks about Judaism as a present reality and not only as a "historical" (and thus superseded) reality. Also to be noted is no. 5 on the complexity of both the historical and the religious relationships between the Church and Judaism. In this same section there is an affirmation that is important for the Catholic Church concerning the centrality of Christ and his unique value in the economy of salvation (no. 7). Clearly this does not mean, however, that the Jews cannot and should not draw salvific gifts from their own traditions. Of course, they can, and should do so.

A *second section* is entitled "Relations between the Old and New Testament". This tries to help put into practice the directions of the Second Vatican Council that call for providing the Catholic faithful with access to a fuller and richer knowledge of Holy Scripture (cf. *Dei Verbum*, 21-22 and *Sacrosanctum Concilium*, 51). This especially includes the Old Testament. It is not always an easy matter to present the relations between both Testaments in a way that fully respects the validity of the Old Testament and shows its permanent usefulness for the Church. At this point, an effort is made to explain the meaning of what is called "typology", since on this a large part of our liturgical use of the Old Testament is grounded. In no way is "typological" usage a devaluation of the validity proper to the Old Testament. Rather to the contrary. One can see this from another angle, since it has always been taught in the Catholic tradition that there is also a "typological" use of the New Testament with respect to the "last things" or eschatological realities (cf. no. 16). The importance of the Old Testament or Judaism is underlined. So, too, is the importance of Jews and Christians hearing the Old Testament together, so that together, in the path opened by the prophetic tradition, we may become more deeply engaged as fellow partisans or humanity today (no 18, 19). The significance of the continuity of the Jewish people in history is again mentioned toward the end of this document (cf. no. 33). It should also be noted that the limits of "typological" usage are acknowledged, and other possible ways of reading the Old Testament in relation to the New are not excluded (cf. no. 11).

The *third section* speaks about the "Jewish Roots of Christianity". Here we turn to the New Testament and try to show that the Jewishness of Jesus and the Judaism of his time are far from being something marginal or incidental. On the contrary, they are connected with the very dynamic of the Incarnation. Thus, they have a specific value in the divine plan of salvation. The relationship of Jesus to the biblical law is carefully assessed (no. 21). So, too, are his relations to the Jewish religious institutions of his time, including the Temple (no. 22). Also carefully assessed are his contacts with the Pharisees, who constituted a movement within the Judaism of his time with which, beyond doubt, he had very close relations and to which he was very near - notwithstanding appearances to the contrary, about which more is said in the subsequent section.

This *fourth section* is, in fact, given over to the problem of the way "The Jews in the New Testament" are presented. On the basis of an exceedingly superficial analysis, some (Jews and Christians) feel that the New Testament is "anti-Semitic". By contrast, in this document the sound and proven results of recent scholarly exegesis are taken into account. Relying on this evidence, principles and criteria are offered to teachers for the presentation and explanation of texts that can create difficulty, whether these are found in the Gospel of John or in other New Testament writings. There is no intention, however, of hiding the fact of the disbelief of Jews in Jesus, a fact which is here called "sad", just as it is in the well-known text of the Letter to the Romans (9:2). In fact, it is also from this point that the division and enmity between Christians and Jews originated, and it is also from this fact that the present urgent need for reconciliation derives, as is very carefully noted (cf. no. 29 D). At the same time, with no less care, it is emphasised that no one can judge the conscience of another, neither of others in the past nor - still less - of others today (*ibid.*, E, F). In this connection, the teaching of the Second Vatican Council on religious liberty must constantly be kept in mind, since this is "one of the bases on which rests the Jewish-Christian dialogue promoted by the Council" (*ibid.*, F). A special paragraph is dedicated to the "delicate question of responsibility for the death of Christ" (no. 30). No attempt is made, however, to enter into complex and difficult historical questions. Rather, in keeping with the viewpoint of the Catechism of the Council of Trent (here quoted explicitly), the text focuses on the theological significance of the death of Christ and our participation in it as sinners. From this perspective, the historical role of "those few Jews" and those few Romans in Jesus' passion becomes a very secondary matter. (The Creed of the Catholic Church has always mentioned Pontius Pilate in relation with the death of Christ, not the Jews).

In the *fifth section*, reference is made to the liturgy and to similarities and points of contact with Jewish worship. Specific mention is made of the source of our prayers, of the cycle of feasts, and of the very structure itself of our Eucharistic prayers.

55

A *sixth section* contains material altogether new in this series of documents. It intends to offer some information on the common history of Judaism and Christianity down through the centuries, a history that unfortunately is largely unknown or poorly understood if not altogether distorted. In this section, the central elements are chiefly three. First, the permanence of Judaism and, as we say, its theological significance, "which allowed Israel to carry to the whole world a witness - often heroic - of its fidelity to the one God" (no. 33). Second, the "religious attachment" of the Jews to the "land of their forefathers", which Christians are encouraged to try to understand (*ibid.*). And third, the creation of the State of Israel. This is taken up with extreme precision. It is said that the "perspective" in which the State should be "envisaged" is not "in itself religious". It should be seen "in ... reference to the common principles of international law" which govern the existence of the various states and their place in the community of nations (*ibid.*). It will surely be noted that for the first time in a document of this Commission, in different but related paragraphs, reference is made to the land and the State. A brief sentence at the end of the paragraph refers to the "extermination" of the Jews (in Hebrew, the *Shoah*, i.e. the catastrophe) during the dark years of the Nazi persecution. It calls upon Catholics to understand how decisive such a tragedy was for the Jews, a tragedy that is also obviously ours. Several teaching aids have been prepared, including those by Catholic offices for education, to help Catholics better comprehend the senseless dimensions of this tragedy and to grasp better its significance. Our Commission is gratified by these efforts and, with this brief emphasis, would like to indicate in them the path to be followed.

Here again (cf. no. 34), as well as toward the beginning of the document (cf. no. 8), the text repeats its condemnation of anti-Semitism. This time, however, that condemnation is explicitly linked with the necessity of a "precise, objective, and rigorously accurate teaching on Judaism", which is the aim of these *Notes*. We are well aware that much has been done to dispel what has been called the "teaching of contempt" (the expression comes from the famous Jewish historian from France, Jules Isaac). But much still remains to be done, not least because new forces of racism and anti-Semitism remain ever ready to rise.

The aim of the *Notes* is, thus, a thoroughly positive one, as the "Conclusion" states. They seek to promote the formation of Catholics equipped "not only for objectivity, justice, and tolerance" (which would already mean a lot), but "also for understanding dialogue". Indeed, "our two traditions are so related that they cannot ignore each other (as is still frequently the case)". It remains a constant necessity that "mutual knowledge... be encouraged at every level".

It is our hope that the in-depth study of this text can be carried out by both parties in an atmosphere free of preconceptions and attentive to meaning and sometimes delicate nuances of many paragraphs. This will help us towards our highly desired goal, which is also the indispensable condition or our united and truly efficacious action together on behalf of the ideals we hold dear and which we have inherited from our shared biblical tradition.

Monsignor Jorge Mejía
Secretary Commission for Religious Relations with the Jews. Rome, June 24, 1985

4. WE REMEMBER: A REFLECTION ON THE SHOAH, ROME, MARCH 16, 1998

VATICAN COMMISSION FOR RELIGIOUS RELATIONS WITH THE JEWS

On numerous occasions during my Pontificate I have recalled with a sense of deep sorrow the sufferings of the Jewish people during the Second World War. The crime which has become known as the *Shoah* remains an indelible stain on the history of the century that is coming to a close.

As we prepare for beginning of the Third Millennium of Christianity, the Church is aware that the joy of a Jubilee is above all the joy that is based on the forgiveness of sins and reconciliation with God and neighbour. Therefore she encourages her sons and daughters to purify their hearts, through repentance of past errors and infidelities. She calls them to place themselves humbly before the Lord and examine themselves on the responsibility which they too have for the evils of our time.

It is my fervent hope that the document: *We Remember: A Reflection on the Shoah*, which the Commission for Religious Relations with the Jews has prepared under your direction, will indeed help to heal the wounds of past misunderstandings and injustices. May it enable memory to play its necessary part in the process of shaping a future in which the unspeakable iniquity of the *Shoah* will never again be possible. May the Lord of history guide the efforts of Catholics and Jews and all men and women of good will as they work together for a world of true respect for the life and dignity of every human being, for all have been created in the image and likeness of God.

From the Vatican, 12 March 1998.

✚ Joannes Paulus II

I. The Tragedy of the Shoah and the Duty of Remembrance

The twentieth century is fast coming to a close and a new Millennium of the Christian era is about to dawn. The 2,000th anniversary of the Birth of Jesus Christ calls all Christians, and indeed invites all men and women, to seek to discern in the passage of history the signs of divine Providence at work, as well as the ways in which the image of the Creator in man has been offended and disfigured.

This reflection concerns one of the main areas in which Catholics can seriously take to heart the summons which Pope John Paul II has addressed to them in his apostolic letter *Tertio Millennio Adveniente*: "It is appropriate that, as the Second Millennium of Christianity draws to a close, the Church should become more fully conscious of the sinfulness of her children, recalling all those times in history when they departed from the spirit of Christ and his Gospel and, instead of offering to the world the witness of a life inspired by the values of faith, indulged in ways of thinking and acting which were truly forms of counter-witness and scandal.[1]

This century has witnessed an unspeakable tragedy, which can never be forgotten: the attempt by the Nazi regime to exterminate the Jewish people, with the consequent killing of millions of Jews. Women and men,

1 Pope John Paul II, Apostolic Letter *Tertio Millennio Adveniente*, 10 November 1994, 33: AAS 87 (1995), 25.

old and young, children and infants, for the sole reason of their Jewish origin, were persecuted and deported. Some were killed immediately, while others were degraded, ill-treated, tortured and utterly robbed of their human dignity, and then murdered. Very few of those who entered the Camps survived, and those who did, remained scarred for life. This was the *Shoah*. It is a major fact of the history of this century, a fact which still concerns us today.

Before this horrible genocide, which the leaders of nations and Jewish communities themselves found hard to believe at the very moment when it was mercilessly being put into effect, no one can remain indifferent, least of all the Church, by reason of her very close bonds of spiritual kinship with the Jewish people and her remembrance of the injustices of the past. The Church's relationship to the Jewish people is unlike the one she shares with any other religion.[2] However, it is not only a question of recalling the past. The common future of Jews and Christians demands that we remember, for "there is no future without memory".[3] History itself is *memoria futuri*.

In addressing this reflection to our brothers and sisters of the Catholic Church throughout the world, we ask all Christians to join us in meditating on the catastrophe which befell the Jewish people, and on the moral imperative to insure that never again will selfishness and hatred grow to the point of sowing such

2 Cf. Pope John Paul II, Speech at the Synagogue of Rome, 13 April 1986, 4; AAS 78 (1986), 1120.
3 Pope John Paul II, Angelus Prayer, 11 June 1995: *Insegnamenti* 181, 1995, 1712).

suffering and death.[4] Most especially, we ask our Jewish friends, "whose terrible fate has become a symbol of the aberrations of which man is capable when he turns against God",[5] to hear us with open hearts.

II. What We Must Remember

While bearing their unique witness to the Holy One of Israel and to the *Torah*, the Jewish people have suffered much at different times and in many places. But the *Shoah* was certainly the worst suffering of all. The inhumanity with which the Jews were persecuted and massacred during this century is beyond the capacity of words to convey. All this was done to them for the sole reason that they were Jews.

The very magnitude of the crime raises many questions. Historians, sociologists, political philosophers, psychologists and theologians are all trying to learn more about the reality of the *Shoah* and its causes. Much scholarly study still remains to be done. But such an event cannot be fully measured by the ordinary criteria of historical research alone. It calls for a "moral and religious memory" and, particularly among Christians, a very serious reflection on what gave rise to it.

The fact that the *Shoah* took place in Europe, that is, in countries of long-standing Christian civilization, raises the question of the relation between the Nazi persecution and the attitudes down the centuries of Christians toward Jews.

4 Cf. Pope John Paul II, Address to Jewish Leaders in Budapest, 18 August 1991, 4; *Insegnamenti* 142, 1991, 349.
5 Pope John Paul II, Encyclical Letter *Centestimus Annus*, 1 May 1991, 17; AAS 83 (1991), 814-815.

III. Relations Between Jews and Christians

The history of relations between Jews and Christians is a tormented one. His Holiness Pope John Paul II has recognised this fact in his repeated appeals to Catholics to see where we stand with regard to our relations with the Jewish people.[6] In effect, the balance of these revelations over 2,000 years has been quite negative.[7]

At the dawn of Christianity, after the crucifixion of Jesus, there arose disputes between the early Church and the Jewish leaders and people who, in their devotion to the Law, on occasion violently opposed the preachers of the Gospel and the first Christians. In the pagan Roman Empire, Jews were legally protected by the privileges granted by the Emperor and the authorities at first made no distinction between Jewish and Christian communities. Soon, however, Christians incurred the persecution of the state. Later, when the Emperors themselves converted to Christianity, they at first continued to guarantee Jewish privileges. But Christian mobs who attacked pagan temples sometimes did the same to synagogues, not without being influenced by certain interpretations of the New Testament regarding the Jewish people as a whole. "In the Christian world - I do not say on the part of the Church as such - erroneous and unjust interpretations of the New Testament regarding the Jewish people and their alleged culpability have circulated for too long,

6   Cf. Pope John Paul II, Address to Delegates of Episcopal Conferences for Catholic-Jewish Relations, 6 March 1982; *Insegnamenti*, 51, 1982, 743-747.

7   Cf. Holy See's Commission for Religious Relations with the Jews, *Notes on the correct way to present the Jews and Judaism in preaching and catechesis in the Roman Catholic Church*, 25 June 1985, VI, 1; Ench. Vat. 9, 1656.

engendering feelings of hostility toward this people".[8] Such interpretations of the New Testament have been totally and definitively rejected by the Second Vatican Council.[9]

Despite the Christian preaching of love for all, even for one's enemies, the prevailing mentality down the centuries penalized minorities and those who were in any way "different". Sentiments of anti-Judaism in some Christian quarters, and the gap which existed between the Church and the Jewish people, led to a generalised discrimination, which ended at times in expulsions or attempts at forced conversions. In a large part of the "Christian" world, at the end of the 18th century, those who were not Christian did not always enjoy a fully guaranteed juridical status. Despite that fact, Jews throughout Christendom held on to their religious traditions and communal customs. They were therefore looked upon with a certain suspicion and mistrust. In times of crisis such as famine, war, pestilence or social tensions, the Jewish minority was sometimes taken as a scapegoat and became the victim of violence, looting, even massacres.

By the end of the 18th century and the beginning of the 19th century, Jews generally had achieved an equal standing with other citizens in most states and a certain number of them held influential positions in society. But in that same historical context, notably in the 19th century, a false and exacerbated nationalism took hold. In a climate of eventful social change, Jews were often accused of exercising an influence dispropor-

8 Cf. Pope John Paul II, Speech to Symposium on the Roots of anti-Judaism, 31 October 1997, 1: *L'Osservatore Romano*, 1 November 1997, p.6.)
9 Cf. Second Vatican Ecumenical Council, *Nostra Aetate*, 4.

tionate to their numbers. Thus there began to spread in varying degrees throughout most of Europe an anti-Judaism that was essentially more sociological and political than religious.

At the same time, theories began to appear which denied the unity of the human race, affirming an original diversity of races. In the 20th century, National Socialism in Germany used these ideas as a pseudo-scientific basis for a distinction between so-called Nordic-Aryan races and supposedly inferior races. Furthermore, an extremist form of nationalism was heightened in Germany by the defeat of 1918 and the demanding conditions imposed by the victors, with the consequence that many saw in National Socialism a solution to their country's problems and co-operated politically with this movement.

The Church in Germany replied by condemning racism. The condemnation first appeared in the preaching of some of the clergy, in the public teaching of the Catholic Bishops, and in the writings of lay Catholic journalists. Already in February and March 1931, Cardinal Bertram of Breslau, Cardinal Faulhaber and the Bishops of Bavaria, the Bishops of the Province of Cologne and those of the Province of Freiburg published pastoral letters condemning National Socialism, with its idolatry of race and of the state.[10] The well-known Advent sermons of Cardinal Faulhaber in 1933, the very year in which National Socialism came to power, at which not just Catholics but also Protestants and Jews were present, clearly expressed rejection of the Nazi anti-Semitic propagan-

10 Cf. B. Statiewki (Ed.), *Akten deutscher Bischofe uber die Lage der Kirche*, 1933-1945, vol. 1, 1933-1934 (Mainz 1968), Appendix.

da.[11] In the wake of the *Kristallnacht*, Bernard Lichtenberg, provost of Berlin Cathedral, offered public prayers for the Jews. He was later to die at Dachau and has been declared Blessed.

Pope Pius XI too condemned Nazi racism in a solemn way in his encyclical *Mit brennender Sorge*,[12] which was read in German churches on Passion Sunday 1937, a step which resulted in attacks and sanctions against members of the clergy. Addressing a group of Belgian pilgrims on 6 September 1938, Pius XI asserted: "Anti-Semitism is unacceptable. Spiritually, we are all Semites".[13] Pius XII, in his very first Encyclical, *Summi Pontificatus*,[14] of 20 October 1939, warned against theories which denied the unity of the human race and against the deification of the state, all of which he saw as leading to a real "hour of darkness".[15]

IV. Nazi Anti-Semitism and the Shoah

Thus we cannot ignore the difference which exists between anti-Semitism based on theories contrary to the constant teaching of the Church on the unity of the human race and on the equal dignity of all races and peoples, and the long-standing sentiments of mistrust and hostility that we call anti-Judaism, of which unfortunately, Christians also have been guilty.

11 Cf. L. Volk, *Der Bayerische Episkopat und der Nationalsozialismus* 1930-1934 (Mainz 1966), pp. 170-174.
12 The Encyclical is dated 14 March 1937; AAS 29 (1937), 145-167.
13 *La Documentation Catholique*, 29 (1938), col. 1460.
14 AAS 31 (1939), 413-453.
15 *Ibid.*, 449.

The National Socialist ideology went even further, in the sense that it refused to acknowledge any transcendent reality as the source of life and the criterion of moral good. Consequently, a human group, and the state with which it was identified, arrogated to itself an absolute status and determined to remove the very existence of the Jewish people, a people called to witness to the one God and the Law of the Covenant. At the level of theological reflection we cannot ignore the fact that not a few in the Nazi party not only showed aversion to the idea of divine Providence at work in human affairs, but gave proof of a definite hatred directed at God himself. Logically, such an attitude also led to a rejection of Christianity, and a desire to see the Church destroyed or at least subjected to the interests of the Nazi state.

It was this extreme ideology which became the basis of the measures taken, first to drive the Jews from their homes and then to exterminate them. The *Shoah* was the work of a thoroughly modern neo-pagan regime. Its anti-Semitism had its roots outside of Christianity and, in pursuing its aims, it did not hesitate to oppose the Church and persecute her members also.

But it may be asked whether the Nazi persecution of the Jews was not made easier by the anti-Jewish prejudices imbedded in some Christian minds and hearts. Did anti-Jewish sentiment among Christians make them less sensitive, or even indifferent, to the persecution launched against the Jews by National Socialism when it reached power?

Any response to this question must take into account that we are dealing with the history of people's attitudes and ways of thinking, subject to multiple influences. Moreover, many people were altogether unaware of the "final solution" that was being put into effect against a whole people; others were afraid for themselves and those near to them, some took advantage of the situation; and still others were moved by envy. A response would need to be given case by case. To do this, however, it is necessary to know what precisely motivated people in a particular situation.

At first the leaders of the Third Reich sought to expel the Jews. Unfortunately, the governments of some Western countries of Christian tradition, including some in North and South America, were more than hesitant to open their borders to the persecuted Jews. Although they could not foresee how far the Nazi hierarchy would go in their criminal intentions, the leaders of those nations were aware of the hardships and dangers to which Jews living in the territories of the Third Reich were exposed. The closing of borders to Jewish emigration in those circumstances, whether due to any anti-Jewish hostility or suspicion, political cowardice or shortsightedness, or national selfishness, lays a heavy burden of conscience on the authorities in question.

In the lands where the Nazis undertook mass deportations, the brutality which surrounded these forced movements of helpless people should have led to suspect the worst. Did Christians give every possible assistance to those being persecuted, and in particular to the persecuted Jews?

Many did, but others did not. Those who did help to save Jewish lives as much as was in their power, even to the point of placing their own lives in danger, must not be forgotten. During and after the war, Jewish communities and Jewish leaders expressed their thanks for all that had been done for them, including what Pope Pius XII did personally or through his representatives to save hundreds of thousands of Jewish lives.[16]

Many Catholic bishops, priests, religious and laity have been honoured for this reason by the State of Israel.

16 The wisdom of Pope Pius XII's diplomacy was publicly acknowledged on a number of occasions by representative Jewish organisations and personalities. For example, on 7 September 1945, Dr. Joseph Nathan, who represented the Italian Hebrew Commission, stated: "Above all, we acknowledge the Supreme Pontiff and the religious men and women who, executing the directives of the Holy Father, recognised the persecuted as their brothers and, with effort and abnegation, hastened to help us, disregarding the terrible dangers to which they were exposed". (*L'Osservatore Romano*, 8 September 1945, p. 2). On 21 September of that same year, Pius XII received in audience Dr. A. Leo Kubowitzki, Secretary General of the World Jewish Congress who came to present "to the Holy Father, in the name of the Union of Israelitic Communities, warmest thanks for the efforts of the Catholic Church on behalf of Jews throughout Europe during the War" (*L'Osservatore Romano*, 23 September 1945, p. 1). On Thursday, 29 November 1945, the Pope met about 60 representatives of Jewish refugees from various concentration camps in Germany, who expressed "their great honour at being able to thank the Holy Father personally for his generosity towards those persecuted during the Nazi-Fascist period" (*L'Osservatore Romano*, 30 November 1945, p. 1). In 1958, at the death of Pope Pius XII, Golda Meir sent an eloquent message: "We share in the grief of humanity. When fearful martyrdom came to our people, the voice of the Pope was raised for its victims. The life of our times was enriched by a voice speaking out about great moral truths above the tumult of daily conflict. We mourn a great servant of peace".

Nevertheless, as Pope John Paul II has recognised, alongside such courageous men and women, the spiritual resistance and concrete action of other Christians was not that which might have been expected from Christ's followers. We cannot know how many Christians in countries occupied or ruled by the Nazi powers or their allies were horrified at the disappearance of their Jewish neighbours and yet were not strong enough to raise their voices in protest. For Christians, this heavy burden of conscience of their brothers and sisters during the Second World War must be a call to penitence.[17]

We deeply regret the errors and failures of those sons and daughters of the Church. We make our own what is said in the Second Vatican Council's declaration *Nostra Aetate*, which unequivocally affirms: *"The Church... mindful of her common patrimony with the Jews, and motivated by the Gospel's spiritual love and by no political considerations, deplores the hatred, persecutions and displays of anti-Semitism directed against the Jews at any time and from any source".*[18]

We recall and abide by what Pope John Paul II, addressing the leaders of the Jewish community in Strasbourg in 1988, stated: *"I repeat again with you the strongest condemnation of anti-Semitism and racism, which are opposed to the principles of Christianity".*[19] The Catholic Church therefore repu-

---

17 Cf. Pope John Paul II, Address to the New Ambassador of the Federal Republic of Germany to the Holy See, 8 November 1990, 2; AAS 83 (1991), 587-588.
18 *Loc.cit.*, no. 4.
19 Address to Jewish Leaders, Strasbourg, 9 October 1988, no. 8; *Insegnamenti* 113, 1988, 1134.

diates every persecution against a people or human group anywhere, at any time. She absolutely condemns all forms of genocide, as well as the racist ideologies that give rise to them. Looking back over this century, we are deeply saddened by the violence that has enveloped whole groups of peoples and nations. We recall in particular the massacre of the Armenians, the countless victims in Ukraine in the 1930's, the genocide of the Gypsies, which was also the result of racist ideas, and similar tragedies which have occurred in America, Africa and the Balkans. Nor do we forget the millions of victims of totalitarian ideology in the Soviet Union, in China, Cambodia and elsewhere. Nor can we forget the drama of the Middle East, the elements of which are well known. Even as we make this reflection "many human beings are still their brothers' victims".[20]

V. Looking Together to a Common Future

Looking to the future of relations between Christians and Jews, in the first place we appeal to our Catholic brothers and sisters to renew the awareness of the Hebrew roots of their faith. We ask them to keep in mind that Jesus was a descendant of David; that the Virgin Mary and the Apostles belonged to the Jewish people; that the Church draws sustenance from the root of that good olive tree onto which have been grafted the wild olive branches of the gentiles (cf. Romans 11:17-24); that the Jews are our dearly beloved brothers, indeed in a certain sense they are "our elder brothers".[21]

20 Pope John Paul II, Address to the Diplomatic Corps, 15 January 1994, 9; AAS 86 (1994), 816.
21 Pope John Paul II, Speech at the Synagogue of Rome, 13 April 1986, 4; AAS 78 (1986), 1120.

At the end of this Millennium the Catholic Church desires to express her deep sorrow for the failures of her sons and daughters in every age. This is an act of repentance (teshuva), since, as members of the Church, we are linked to the sins as well as the merits of all her children. The Church approaches with deep respect and great compassion the experience of extermination, the Shoah, suffered by the Jewish people during World War II. It is not a matter of mere words, but indeed of binding commitment. *"We would risk causing the victims of the most atrocious deaths to die again if we do not have an ardent desire for justice, if we do not commit ourselves to insure that evil does not prevail over good as it did for millions of children of the Jewish people... Humanity cannot permit all that to happen again".*[22]

We pray that our sorrow for the tragedy which the Jewish people has suffered in our century will led to a new relationship with the Jewish people. We wish to turn awareness of past sins into a firm resolve to build a new future in which there will be no more anti-Judaism among Christians or anti-Christian sentiment among Jews, but rather a shared mutual respect, as befits those who adore the one Creator and Lord and have a common father in faith, Abraham.

Finally, we invite all men and women of good will to reflect deeply on the significance of the Shoah. The victims from their graves, and the survivors through the vivid testimony of what they have suffered, have become a loud voice calling the attention of all humanity. To remember this terrible experience is to become

22 Pope John Paul II, Address on the occasion of a commemoration of the *Shoah*, 7 April 1994, 3; *Insegnamenti* 171, 1994, 897 and 893.

fully conscious of the salutary warning it entails: the spoiled seeds of anti-Judaism and anti-Semitism must never again be allowed to take root in any human heart.

PRESENTATION BY CARDINAL
EDWARD IDRIS CASSIDY

The Holy See has to date published, through its Commission for Religious Relations with the Jews, two significant documents intended for the application of the Second Vatican Council's Declaration *Nostra Aetate*, No. 4; the 1974 *Guidelines and Suggestions*; and the 1985 *Notes on the Correct Way to Present the Jews and Judaism in Preaching and Catechesis in the Catholic Church*.

Today it publishes another document, which the Holy See's Commission on Religious Relations with the Jews has prepared at the express request of His Holiness Pope John Paul II. This document, which contains a reflection on the *Shoah*, is another step on the path marked out by the Second Vatican Council in our relations with the Jewish people. In the words which His Holiness wrote in his letter to me as President of the Commission, it is our fervent hope "that the document [....] will help to heal the wounds of past misunderstandings and injustices".[1]

It is addressed to the Catholic faithful throughout the world, not only in Europe where the *Shoah* took place, hoping that all Christians will join their Catholic brothers and sisters in meditating on the catastrophe which befell the Jewish people, on its causes, and on the moral imperative to ensure that never again such a tragedy will happen. At the same time it asks our Jewish friends to hear us with an open heart.

On the occasion of a meeting in Rome on 31 August 1987 of representatives of the Holy See's Commission

1 The letter of His Holiness dated 12 March 1998.

73

for Religious Relations with the Jews and of the International Jewish Committee on Interreligious Consultations, the then President of the Holy See's Commission for Religious Relations with the Jews, Cardinal Johannes Willebrands, announced the intention of the Commission to prepare an official Catholic document on the *Shoah*. The following day, 1 September 1987, the participants of this meeting were received at Castel Gandolfo by His Holiness Pope John Paul II, who affirmed the importance of the proposed document for the Church and for the world. His Holiness spoke of his personal experience in his native country and his memories of living close to a Jewish community now destroyed. He recalled a recent address to the Jewish community in Warsaw, in which he spoke of the Jewish people as a *force of conscience* in the world today and of the Jewish memory of the *Shoah* as "a warning, a witness, and a silent cry" to all humanity. Citing the Exodus of the Jewish people from Egypt as a paradigm and a continuing source of hope, His Holiness expressed his deep conviction that, with God's help, evil can be overcome in history, even the awesome evil of the *Shoah*.

We can read in the Joint Press Communique which was released at that time, that the Jewish delegations warmly welcomed the initiative of an official Catholic document on the *Shoah*, and expressed the conviction that such a document will contribute significantly to combating attempts to revise and to deny the reality of the *Shoah* and to trivialize its religious significance for Christians, Jews, and humanity.

In the years following the announcement, the Holy See's Commission for Religious Relations with the

Jews engaged in a process of consciousness-raising and of reflection on several levels in the Catholic Church, and in different places.

In the *Guidelines and Suggestions or Implementing the Conciliar Declaration Nostra Aetate*, No. 4, published on 1 December 1974, the Holy See's Commission recalled that "the step taken by the Council finds its historical setting in circumstances deeply affected by the memory of the persecution and massacre of Jews which took place in Europe, just before and during the Second World War". Yet, as the Guidelines pointed out, "the problem of Jewish-Christian relations concerns the Church as such, since it is when 'pondering her own mystery' (*Nostra Aetate*, no. 4) that she encounters the mystery of Israel. Therefore, even in areas where no Jewish communities exist, this remains an important problem".

Pope John Paul II himself has repeatedly called upon us to see where we stand with regard to our relations with the Jewish people. In doing so, "we must remember how much the balance (of these relations) over two thousand years has been negative".[2] This long period "which", in the words of Pope John Paul II, "we must not tire of reflecting upon in order to draw from it the appropriate lessons"[3] has been marked by many manifestations of anti-Judaism and anti-Semitism, and, in this century, by the horrifying events of the *Shoah*.

2 Cf. Notes on the Correct Way to Present the Jews and Judaism in Preaching and Catechesis in the Catholic Church (24 June 1985).
3 Speech delivered on the occasion of His Holiness to the Synagogue of Rome (13 April 1986), 4: AAS 78 (1986), 1120.

Therefore, the Catholic Church wants all Catholics, and indeed all people, everywhere, to know about this. It does so also with the hope that it will help Catholics and Jews towards the realisation of those universal goals that are found in their common roots. In fact, this burden should be a call to repentance. As His Holiness has put it on one occasion, "guilt must always be the point of departure for conversion".

We are confident that all the Catholic faithful in every part of the world will be helped by this document to discover in their relationship with the Jewish people "the boldness of brotherhood".[4]

4 Pope John Paul II in his address to the Diplomatic Corps on 15 January 1994.

BIBLIOGRAPHY

DOCUMENTS

Helga Croner, (editor), **Stepping Stones to Further Jewish-Christian Relations**, (1977) **More Stepping Stones to Jewish Christian Relations**, (unabridged collections of Christian Documents 1975-1985) (Paulist Press, New York, 1985)

The Theology of the Churches and the Jewish People, (Statements by the World Council of Churches and its Member Churches), (W.C.C. Publications, Geneva, 1988)

Guidelines for Catholic-Jewish Relations, (on the Liturgy), Committee for Catholic-Jewish Relations of the Bishops' Conference of England and Wales, (CTS Publications, London, 1988)

Christians and Jews, A New Way of Thinking, Guidelines for the Churches, (The Churches' Commission for Inter-Faith Relations, Council of Churches for Britain & Ireland)

Subsequent documents are published as issued in periodicals:

S.I.D.I.C. A review published 3 times a year in Rome on matters related to Jewish-Christian dialogue. Subscriptions: Clare Jardine, Study Centre for Christian Jewish Relations, 17, Chepstow Villas, London W11 3DZ

Briefing, The official documentation and information service of the Catholic Bishops' Conferences of England & Wales and Scotland, Subscriptions to:

77

Catholic Media Trust, Redemptorist Convent, Back Gilmoss Lane, Liverpool L11 OAY

Information Service, The Pontifical Council for Promoting Christian Unity, via del 'Erba, 00193 Rome, Italy

Other periodicals with an interest in Jewish-Christian matters)

Common Ground, The Council of Christians and Jews, Drayton House, 30 Gordon St., London WC1H OAN

Current Dialogue, Inter-Religious Relations, World Council of Churches, 150 Route de Ferney, PO Box 2100, 1211 Geneva, Switzerland

BOOKS
Judaism, The New Testament and Early Christianity

Charlesworth James H. ed. **Jesus' Jewishness: Exploring the Place of Jesus Within Early Judaism**, (Crossroad, New York, 1991)

Jesus Within Judaism, (S.P.C.K., London, 1989)

Dunn James D. G., **The Partings of the Ways: Between Christianity and Judaism and their significance for the character of Christianity**, (S.C.M. Press, London, 1991)

Efroymson David, Fisher Eugene J., Klenicki Leon, eds. **Within Context: Essays on Jews and Judaism**

78

in the **New Testament**, (Liturgical Press, Collegeville, 1993)

Fisher Eugene J. ed., **The Jewish Roots of Christian Liturgy** (Paulist Press, N.Y. 1990)

Harrington David J. **God's People in Christ** (Fortress Press, 1980)
Paul on the Mystery of Israel, (Liturgical Press/Michael Glazier, Collegeville, 1992)

Hilton Michael & Marshall Gordian, **The Gospels and Rabbinic Judaism: A Study Guide**, (S.C.M. Press, London, 1988)

Lachs Samuel T., **A Rabbinic Commentary on the New Testament: The Gospels of Matthew, Mark and Luke,** (KTAV Publishing House/ADL, New Jersey, 1987)

Perelmuter Hayim G., **Siblings: Rabbinic Judaism and Early Christianity at their Beginnings**, (Paulist Press, N.Y., 1989)

Rivkin Ellis, **What Crucified Jesus? Messianism, Pharisaism, and the Development of Christianity**, (UHAC Press, N.Y., 1997)

Sanders E.P. **Jesus and Judaism**, (S.C.M. Press, London 1985)
Paul and Palestinian Judaism, (S.C.M. Press, London, 1977)

Sanders Jack T., **The Jews in Luke-Acts**, (S.C.M. Press, 1987)

Sandmel Samuel, **Judaism and Christian Beginnings**, (O.U.P., 1978)

Smiga George M., **Pain and Polemic: Anti-Judaism in the Gospels**, (Paulist Pres, N.Y., 1992)

Vermes Geza, **Jesus the Jew**, (Fontana, Collins, London 1973)
Jesus and the World of Judaism, The Religion of Jesus the Jew, (S.C.M. Press, London, 1983, 1993)

Williamson Clark M. & Allen Ronald J., **Interpreting Difficult Texts: Anti-Judaism and Christian Preaching**, (S.C.M. Press, London 1989)

Wilson Marvin R., **Our Father Abraham: Jewish Roots of the Christian Faith**, (Eerdmans, Grand Rapids, 1989)

Wylen Stephen M., **The Jews in the Time of Jesus: An Introduction**, (Paulist Press, N.Y., 1996)

JEWISH-CHRISTIAN RELATIONS IN HISTORY
Anti-Judaism/Anti-Semitism
Beck Norman A., **Mature Christianity in the 21st Century (The Recognition and Repudiation of the Anti-Jewish Polemic in the New Testament)**, (Crossroad, N.Y., 1994)

Davies Alan T., **Anti-Semitism and the Foundations of Christianity**, (Paulist Press, 1979)

Flannery Edward J., **The Anguish of the Jews: Twenty-Three Centuries of Anti-Semitism**, (Paulist Press, N.Y., 1985)

Gager John G., **The Origins of Anti-Semitism**, (Oxford University Press, 1983)

Klein Charlotte, **Anti-Judaism in Christian Theology**, (S.P.C.K. London 1978)

Saperstein Marc, **Moments of Crisis in Jewish-Christian Relations**, (S.C.M. Press, London, 1990)

The Shoah (Holocaust)

Berkovits Eliezer, **Faith after the Holocaust**, (KTAV Publishing House, N.Y. 1973)

Cohn-Sherbok Dan, **Holocaust Theology**, (Lamp Press, London 1989)

Eckardt Alice L. & Roy, **A Long Night's Journey Into Day**, (Pergamon Press, Oxford, 1988)

Fleischner Eva, ed., **Auschwitz, Beginning of a New Era**, (KTAV Publishing House, N.Y., 1974)

Gilbert Martin, **Atlas of the Holocaust**, (Michael Joseph. London, 1982)
The Holocaust: The Jewish Tragedy, (Collins, 1986)

Gottlieb Roger S. ed., **Thinking the Unthinkable: Meanings of the Holocaust**, (Paulist Press, N.Y., 1990)

Landau Ronnie S., **Studying the Holocaust, Issues, Readings and Documents**, (Routledge, London, 1998)

Wiesel Elie, **Gates of the Forest**, (Holt, Rinehart & Winston, N.Y., 1966)

Ongoing History:

Bradshaw Paul F. & Hoffman Lawrence A. eds., **The Making of Jewish and Christian Worship**, (University of Notre Dame Press, 1991)

Edwards John, **The Jews in Christian Europe**, 1400-1700, (Routledge, London, 1988)

Fisher Eugene J. ed., **Interwoven Destinies: Jews and Christians Through the Ages**, (Paulist Press, N.Y., 1993)

McInnes Val A. OP ed., **New Visions: Historical & Theological Perspectives on the Jewish-Christian Dialogue**, (Crossroad, N.Y., 1993)

Perry Marvin & Schweitzer Frederick M. eds., **Jewish-Christian Encounters over the Centuries**, (Peter Lang, N.Y. etc., 1994)

Shanks Hershel, ed. **Christianity and Rabbinic Judaism: A Parallel History of their Origins and Early Development**, (S.P.C.K., London,1993)

Shermis Michael & Zannoni Arthur E. eds., **Introduction to Jewish-Christian Relations**, (Paulist Press, N.Y.,1991)

Wilken Robert L., **The Land Called Holy: Palestine in Christian History and Thought**, (Yale University Press, New Haven & London, 1993)

The Contemporary Dialogue

Bayfield Tony & Braybrooke M. eds., **Dialogue With a Difference**, (S.C.M. Press, London, 1992)

Braybrooke Marcus, **Time to Meet: Towards a Deeper Relationship between Jews and Christians**, (S.C.M. Press, London, 1990)

Burrell David & Landau Yehezkel, eds., **Voices from Jerusalem**, (Paulist Press, N.Y. 1992)

Cohen Martin A. & Croner H. eds., **Christian Mission/Jewish Mission**, (Paulist Press, N.Y., 1982)

Fisher Eugene J. & Rudin James, eds., **Twenty Years of Jewish-Catholic Relations**, (Paulist Press, N.Y., 1986)

Fisher Eugene J. & Klenicki Leon, eds., **In Our Time: The Flowering of Jewish-Catholic Dialogue**, (Paulist Press, N.Y. 1990)

Fisher Eugene J. & Klenicki Leon, ed. **Spiritual Pilgrimage: Texts on Jews and Judaism 1979-1995, Pope John Paul II**, (Crossroad, N.Y., 1996)

Fisher Eugene J. ed., **Visions of the Other: Jewish and Christian Theologians Assess the Dialogue**, (Paulist Press, N.Y., 1994)

International Catholic-Jewish Liaison Committee, **Fifteen Years of Catholic-Jewish Dialogue**, 1970-1985, (Libreria Editrice Lateranense & Libreria Editrice Vaticana, 1988)

Kenny Anthony, **Catholics, Jews and the Land of Israel**, (Paulist Press, N.Y. 1993)

Klenicki Leon, **Towards a Theological Encounter: Jewish Understandings of Christianity**, (Paulist Press, N.Y., 1991)

Klenicki Leon & Huck Gabe, eds., **Spirituality and Prayer: Jewish & Christian Understandings**, (Paulist Press, N.Y.1983)

Klenicki Leon & Wigoder Geoffrey, eds., **A Dictionary of the Jewish-Christian Dialogue**, (Paulist Press, N.Y., 1984, expanded 1995)

Mussner Franz, **Tractate on the Jews: The Significance of Judaism for Christian Faith**, (S.P.C.K. London, 1984)

Pawlikowski John, **Christ in the Light of the Jewish-Christian Dialogue**, (Paulist Press, N.Y., 1982)

Pawlikowski John, **Jesus and the Theology of Israel**, (Michael Glazier, Wilmington, Delaware, 1989)

Thomas Clemens, **A Christian Theology of Judaism**, (Paulist Press, N.Y., 1980)

Thomas Clemens, & Wyschogrod Michael, eds., **Understanding Scripture Explorations of Jewish & Christian Traditions of Interpretation**, (Paulist Press, N.Y., 1987)

van Buren Paul, **A Theology of the Jewish-Christian Reality**, (3 vols.) (Harper & Row, San Francisco, London etc., 1980- 1988)

Willebrands Johannes, Cardinal, **Church and the Jewish People: New Considerations**, (Paulist Press, N.Y. 1992)

JUDAISM

Gilbert Martin, **Jewish Historical Atlas**, (Weidenfeld and Nicolson, London, 1972)

Jacobs Louis, **A Jewish Theology**, (Darton, Longman & Todd, 1973)

Sacks Jonathan, **The Persistence of Faith**, (Weidenfeld & Nicolson, London 1991)

Solomon Norman, **Judaism: A Very Short Introduction**, (Oxford University Press, 1996)

Unterman A., **Jews: Their Religious Beliefs and Practices**, (Routledge & Kegan Paul, London, 1981)

Wittenberg Jonathan, **The Three Pillars of Judaism: A Search for Faith and Values**, (S.C.M. Press, London, 1996)

JEWS IN BRITAIN

Brook Stephen, **The Club: The Jews of Modern Britain**, (Constable, London, 1989)

Cesarini David, ed., **The Making of Modern Anglo-Jewry**, (Basil Blackwell, London 1990)

Fletcher Jones Pamela, **The Jews of Britain**, (Windrush Press, Gloucester, 1990)

Lipman V. D. **A History of the Jews in Britain Since 1858**, (Leicester University Press, 1990)

85

ZIONISM AND ISRAEL

Goldberg David J., **To the Promised Land, A History of Zionist Thought**, (Penguin Books, London, 1996)

Hertzberg Arthur, **The Zionist Idea**, (Schocken Books, N.Y., 1991)

Merkley Paul C., **The Politics of Christian Zionism 1891-1948**, (Frank Cass, London, 1998)

Pragai Michael, **Faith and Fulfilment: Christians and the Return to the Promised Land**, (Valentine, Mitchell, London 1985)

Sachar Howard M., **A History of Israel**, (Knopf, N.Y. 1979 Vol.2 (from 1973, Oxford University Press, 1987)

CENTRES FOR INFORMATION AND ADVICE

Board of Deputies of British Jews
5th Floor, Commonwealth House, 1-19 New Oxford
Street, London WC1A 1NF
Tel: (0171) 543 5400
Departments for advice and help:
Central Jewish Lecture and Information,
Education and Youth
Central Enquiry Desk: Tel: *(0171) 543 5421*

Council of Christians and Jews
Drayton House, 30 Gordon Street,
London WC1H OAN
Tel: (0171) 388 3305
(lectures, conferences, publications etc.)

Jewish Educational Bureau
8 Westcombe Avenue, Leeds LS8 2BS,
Tel: (0113) 2663613
Catalogue of resources available.

Study Centre for Christian-Jewish Relations
17 Chepstow Villas, London W11 3DZ
Tel: (0171) 727 3597
Advice, speakers available, programmes organised,
list of publications on the background to the Gospels
and early Church.